The Fathers We Find

THE MAKING OF A PLEASANT, HUMBLE BOY

CHARLES P. RIES

BAD MONK
productions

BAD MONK
productions

. . . .

Front cover design: Mike Pavelich- www.mitegraphics.com
Book design: Lucia Lozano- www.process2creative.com

Printed and manufactured in the United States of America

First Edition: 2015

Library of Congress Control Number: 2015947189

ISBN 978-0-692-48138-7

. . . .

To my folks.

Contents

1. Holy Water   3

2. When Memories Begin   6

3. He Answered Their Prayers   13

4. A Call to Cleanliness   34

5. The Big Two   40

6. Fish Creek   50

7. I Dare You   66

8. Bill The Mink   88

9. The Wisdom of the River   105

10. Catholic Boy   120

11. Thrifty Pete   139

12. Dad Drives   160

13. Eight Quarts of Milk   169

14.	Bigger Than Life	180
15.	High School	189
16.	The Lesson	207
17.	Birdman	224
18.	The 360-Degree Pee	236
19.	Love Lost	242
20.	Mr. Spock	261
21.	Night Crawlers	274
22.	Black River	284

| *The Author* | 291 |
| *Praise for* The Fathers We Find | 293 |

．．．

BEYOND *the predictability of my father's work and prayer habits, there was one ritual he performed without fail. He blessed our beds. Each night after he'd washed and prayed, he'd come up to the two bedrooms on the second level of our home and make the sign of the cross over his children as they lay sleeping. Carrying a small glass bottle with a cross etched on the front, he sprinkled us with holy water. In his mind, he was showering us with a protective blanket of grace that would fill our room with angels and hover over us until morning. Most nights I was already fast asleep when he made his rounds, but on occasion just as sleep neared, I would feel a drop of holy water fall on my face or hand. It was a good feeling. An act of love that made the night safe. This rite of passage into the night was as sure as the sun rising in the morning. He'd silently come into the room I shared with my three brothers and bless our two beds. My father's world was built on routines and rituals. They kept his feet on the ground. They made the world a safe predictable place for him and for us. In these silent acts of kindness he extended his heart. These were the hugs and kisses he never shared with us. Through this twilight ritual he came as close to touching our souls as he ever would and ever did.*

1.

Holy Water

I'D GO through the same routine every time I visited. I'd tell him I loved him and then sit in silence looking at him. Waiting for him to say something. I wanted to run, but I owed it to him to stay there and say the words. He had earned at least that much respect. I repeated, "Dad, I love you," one final time and saw what I thought was a trickle of tears coming from his eyes as he sat hunched and strapped in his wheelchair, unable to talk, his body shaking uncontrollably. I wasn't sure if what I saw was the disease or a moment of real feeling. I had long given up on him, but still held out for a sign. I waited for the feelings buried deep within him to finally come out and breathe the same air with me.

As tears rolled down his cheeks I was certain I had finally seen him. I was certain that the curtain of his disease had parted for a moment and he was sharing something real with me. The view made me pity him all the more, but I could not reach down and find tears for him. I had stopped crying years ago. I would not weep for him now.

After a series of small strokes and following the administration of the Last Rites, he mercifully died. His eighty-eight year life was over. *What am I to feel? How am I to be? It's my father, who just died.* But I felt nothing. He had taught me well. I now had a firm grip on my feelings. They were stored a million miles away where they could do me no harm.

. . .

My father was not a warm and fuzzy kind of guy, my brother Joe began his eulogy. *He wasn't a very playful person—he taught us how to work and all of my brothers and sisters know how to do that very well. I've learned some things are more important than being able to tell a good story or being able to entertain friends—things like integrity, sincerity, decency—in other words, faithfulness to one's beliefs.*

I waited for something to open me up. For some sweet memory to find me and send me my tears, but nothing came. I was still angry with him. Angry that I had to shut myself down. Angry that I couldn't remember him hugging or comprehending me. I had no connection with this man other than the holy water he sprinkled on my bed each night.

Every Tuesday night and often on Sunday, my dad would go to St. Vincent de Paul meetings and then would go out to visit and help families in need. My dad wasn't a do-gooder though because that implies superficiality. What he did, he did from his heart. He did what he did because of a deeply held belief that it was just the right thing to do.

As my brother continued, I stopped listening. I withdrew and looked forward to the after-burial luncheon and drinking a few Brandy Old Fashions to my old man, the best minker that ever lived.

2.

When Memories Begin

WITH closed eyes, I reached back and searched for my memories. The meaning of who I had become would be discovered by carefully remembering these building blocks of my nature.

A series of snapshots, smells, colors and dreams passed before me—the mysterious pieces of a boy on the verge of becoming. Splashing in a puddle created by a late August storm with my younger brother. Feeling the close quarters of my dad's 1949 Buick as the nine of us crowd together en route to my Uncle's for Easter Sunday dinner. Abducting my aunt's poppy seed tort from the dessert table and carrying it into a nearby clothes closet so I could have all its creamy goodness to myself and then crying hysterically as my mother discovered me and liberated my friend from my intoxicated fingers.

Snapshots. Fragments of memory.

Green farm fields. The chirping of my father's mink after weaning and the smell of pelting season. Snow forts, ice-skating in the swamp and my mother's garden with its raspberries, strawberries, rhubarb and vegetables. The smell of bread baking in the kitchen. A world of constancy nestled in the heart of Wisconsin.

Our red brick house that stood next to my grand-parent's cream brick home. And next to our home my uncle's and just thirty feet further south my aunt's. We'd laughed and called it Riesville. Four homes along a black top country road populated with seventeen children and eight adults. The only things that ever changed were the weather, the seasons and our ages.

It felt as if we had always been here. My ancestors homesteaded this land in 1830. Fresh off the boat from Luxemburg, my great great grandparents bought their stake in America. Two more generations of dairy farmers followed and then came my father who would raise mink rather than dairy cattle. Hardworking, church-going, frugal men and women who made good use of their time on earth.

The earliest days of my life were without surprise or pain. There was nothing to distinguish one day from the other. Until my eyes started to open and as natural as life itself, I began to see. And the life I remember began.

. . .

"Chucky, is the mail truck here yet?" my mother called from the kitchen.

"Not yet. I'm watching," I called back. My nose pressed against the window that looked north toward my grandparent's house. Their home, and Riesville's large postal box, stood beneath an Oak Tree whose branches reached like protecting arms over the sky blue roof and soft yellow brick exterior of their house.

"Well, it'll be here in a minute or two," she replied.

I was old enough for my first chore. At four years old I was now big enough to find a place in the factory of my father's farm.

"I can see it! I see the mail truck," I shouted as I raced through the kitchen and out the back door, running with short urgent strides, propelling myself along a foot-worn path that carried me and a procession of mail collectors before me through a sparse orchard of crab apple trees toward the mailbox into which all of the mail destined for Riesville was placed.

"You must be the new delivery boy?" a voice called to me from the mail truck.

"Yes sir. It's my job."

"Think you can carry all this stuff? You're just a little guy," I heard the voice say as a tanned arm reached out of the side window and placed the day's news, bills and letters into my outstretched arms.

It was the commencement of my working life. It was the day I became a little man.

"Well, look who's here," I heard my grandmother Mary say as I opened the screen door leading to her kitchen. "So, you're in charge now, huh?" she said in her thick German accent.

"I'm in charge of mail," I replied, holding the overflowing bundle. Hugging it and making sure not one item escaped my embrace.

"I see that. Well, you just put the mail there on the table and sit down," she said, pointing to the chair where she wanted her grandson to sit. "You look hungry. You have three more houses to go before lunchtime. You need some apple pie," she said in a way that always sounded like an order.

"Grandma, I have mail to deliver now," I tried to explain, letting her know I knew my job.

"You will. But first you get some pie. You work. You

eat. Little men have to eat," she said, placing a wedge of pie in front of me from one of the four she'd set on the table to cool. It was my diploma to manhood—a quarter-pan-man-sized certificate of achievement. As I sat and took a fork full of the warm treat, I realized I wouldn't complete my route until I'd finished her pie. As I ate, she talked to me in her short matter-of-fact sentences. "God gave us a good day. A good day for picking raspberries and canning tomatoes," she said as she sorted the mail, not looking up until she had placed the day's delivery onto four neat piles. She tied each pile with a piece of butcher's twine and then took a long admiring look at the young man sitting at her table and nodded affirmatively, mentally noting that he was right on track to becoming a good, productive little Ries. Her gift of pie was God smiling on my life.

As I neared the end of my sweet tribute the phone rang, "Yes, Chucky's here. Sure, he'll have plenty of room for lunch. He's busy with grandma now. We're talking. We have business to do. He'll be home soon. He has mail to deliver," she said to my mother who'd called wondering where the new mail carrier had disappeared. With my plate now spotless, I got up and received an uncharacteristic hug from my grandmother and resumed my route. She'd laid the three bundles of mail in my arms, "you get moving now. Your mom's got your lunch waiting. Scoot."

I bounded out of the kitchen and saw my grandfather Peter coming up the gravel road that lead to the carpenter shop, "better get moving Chucky, everyone's wondering if the mailman thought you were a letter and mailed you to Green Bay."

"Okay grandpa, I'm moving now. Grandma had pie for me."

"I'm sure of that," he said as he watched me make my way back along the path, through the orchard and over a wide mowed field where we played softball.

I walked the final hundred yards to the far end of Riesville where I delivered my aunt's and then my uncle's mail. Knocking on each door, handing the bundle through the opening to a, "thanks Chucky, you want to stay for lunch."

"Nope. I had pie at grandma's. Now I have to get home for lunch," I said as I sped back across the softball field and entered the kitchen where my six siblings were already halfway through with their meal.

"All done?" my mother asked.

"Yup, done for this day."

Well, take a seat and have some lunch or did Grandma fill you full of pie?" she said, seeing the telltale sign of early dessert on the corners of my mouth and clinging to the front of my shirt.

It was my first day of work and my life's first memory.

3.

He Answered Their Prayers

"DEAR God, if it be Your will, let this child become a soldier in your army. Let him serve You. Let me be a vessel for Thy holy goodness," my mother prayed each morning at early mass. A young woman in her early thirties, Helen Ries had just given birth to the first of what would be seven children. Small and tireless, she made time amidst her full workday to pray. She was a born multi-tasker. She could pray while scrubbing the floor, boiling potatoes, and darning socks. But she was a dim light when compared to my father's omnipotence. He prayed three times a day—morning, noon, and night—on his knees. He prayed in the car when he passed a church, tipping his hat to the body and blood of Christ that lie entombed in the ornate tabernacle at its center. He'd pull his rosary out from its leather pouch for a quick round just because it felt good. He was a man with his eye on the eternal prize. Carl Ries knew this life was just a stopping-off place to the big prize that lies on the other side.

My parents were so good at praying that God answered their prayers and, in so doing, set in motion a miraculous series of events. Their firstborn child became a priest. But Helen and Carl Ries did not stop there. They continued to pray, and God granted their wish five more times, sending six of their seven children to the convent or seminary.

I was born twelve years after my oldest brother Bob. While I was in the numinous state of infant survival, Bob was heading off to Seminary High School.

No one found it peculiar that fourteen year olds were making career decisions and going off into the wild blue yonder of service to God. Unlike parents today, who coddle their progeny long after college, Carl and Helen Ries never gave a second thought to their young children signing up to serve the Lord. They believed God spoke most clearly to the young, whose hearts were free of sin.

I watched my elder siblings begin their religious careers with a series of eighth grade graduation parties.

The Ries Family was setting new records in religious vocations. The church elders sat back in beatific amazement. Of course, some were jealous. Our pew neighbor, Mrs. Lilac Rummelfinger, was one who coveted the Ries' family record.

Lilac always sat exactly three pews behind us. Among the faithful, all the sitting locations were as fixed as concrete. People seemed to grow out of the pews like blessed seeds and mature into God-fearing adults after many years of worship. There they were and there they had always been. Lilac was no different. She was so fervent in her prayer and song that I often sensed the back of my head heating up from the sanctified emissions pouring forth from her devotion.

A prayerful woman in her mid-sixties, Lilac loved the church. Each Sunday she'd show up wearing the same blue floral print dress and an attractive velvet forest green hat, accentuated by two extremely long pheasant tail feathers. My brother Joe and I had to be careful when she turned her head so she didn't swat us or tickle our noses with her decorative feathers. Her excessive face powder made her appear a bit ghostlike, but with liberal blood red lipstick and rouge, she was quite the stunning church lady.

Lilac lived for the Lord. Daily mass, the parish

council, charity guilds, and religion classes were her labors of love. Through them she served her God and community. One had to wonder whether the departure of her late husband Leonard, due to a sudden and unexpected heart attack, hadn't resulted in Lilac redirecting her considerable female passions toward an equally passionate relationship with the Lord.

My parents were exchanging the usual pleasantries at the end of mass one day when Lilac approached them. "Not one priest or nun in my family, but look at you. You have a son and a daughter already pledged to the Lord and another daughter who's signing up next month. I pray. I pray darn hard, but God doesn't seem to answer my prayers. For some reason He's chosen to ignore His Lilac. But I haven't lost hope. I just keep praying," she said as she gazed longingly at our holy family.

"Well, congratulations," Lilac said. "I think it's great that your third oldest is going to join the Carmelites. What an amazing record. How many does that make— three? You must be very proud to have Bob, Kathleen, and now Sue head off to serve the Lord. If I could have had just one of my five children answer the call, I'd be head over heels with joy. Don't know why God's ignoring Lilac Rummerfinger. You two have so much to be proud of, and to think you have four more children to go," she said peering around my mother to get a better view of the next four Ries priests. "Four more opportunities to praise the Lord with action," she concluded.

"Well, Lilac, we're sort of hoping a few will get married, so we'll have some grandchildren. But if God wants to take them all, who are we to question His will?" my mother said. "Still, I'd like a few grandchildren," she repeated, feeling just a bit selfish for asking that a couple of her children lead secular lives.

"That would be nice," Lilac said. "Still, it seems unfair that almost every religious vocation coming out of this congregation in the last six years are all your children. I mean, don't you think the Lord should spread His grace around a little bit?" she concluded as she waved and walked off muttering to herself about the unfathomable mysteries of God's mind.

As a small child I witnessed hundreds of these congratulatory exchanges following mass. I could feel the disbelief that lay beneath the praise and smiles of my parents' worshipful friends. We weren't just special. We were a living family miracle.

By the age of five, I began to pray that I too would become a priest someday. But I worried that my collective sins—small though they may be—would be too great for God to hear my prayer. I wanted to please the Lord. I could see the proud glow in my parents' eyes whenever Bob came home from the seminary. He was their prize, the standard by which we were measured. There was no other career option in my family; I had to become a priest.

. . .

Birth order experts speculate that children born four to five years following the arrival of an elder sibling accrue all of the same benefits that eldest or only children do. They theorize this birthing pause allows the mother to recharge her hormones and the family to direct all its nurturing energy toward this child as they would an only or firstborn child. Armchair sociologists say only and oldest children are brighter, more successful, and more likely to get ahead in the world. So my arrival four years after my brother Jim had set the stage for my greatness. Unlike my elder siblings who arrived in quick succession, I would be special and, as the baby of the family, placed on the Gerber Baby pedestal of worship. Into me would pour the adulation of five older siblings and two adoring parents. Into me a horde of cousins, aunts, uncles, and grandparents would impart their collective wisdom. I would be the center of attention. I would be confident. I would be successful.

But such greatness was to be snatched from my chubby little hands by the remarkable fertility of my parents. I would enjoy firstborn status for a mere thirteen months, as my brother Joe rolled off the assembly line to bump me from my pedestal. He would forever be the cute little baby, while I would struggle for my place in the sun, grabbing for whatever crumbs of attention I could. I became the family crumb-grabber.

I suppose I was lucky that my sisters, Sue and Kathleen, who were ten and twelve years older than me, could give me the kind of attention my overworked mother had no time for. Perhaps being raised by my loving sisters, both children themselves, delayed my development, and maybe this was my salvation. This once-removed parenting formula gave me a little breathing room from the rigid expectations of my family. I could live a little closer to the edge, while my younger brother, who glowed in the family spotlight, would be expected to toe the line.

As the proverbial *Irish Twins*, Joe and I experienced everything together. We shared the same bed until our early teens. Our bed and the one my older brothers Jim and John shared were in the same small room in the too small house my father built. The room was exactly big enough to hold two full beds and a tiny dresser that all four of us shared. We were a close family, literally, and when it came to housing, my father was thrifty.

After years of begging for more space and a few modern conveniences, he begrudgingly conceded to my mother's pleas for an additional bathroom. Being a rustic minimalist, he located the second shower and toilet in the fruit cellar.

Our fruit cellar was a cool, dim, and damp place, perfect for keeping fruits and vegetables from ripening too quickly. It had a rough concrete floor, an unfinished ceiling, and shelves lining the walls on which my mother stored the canned fruits and vegetables she made each year. In such a place, the hapless bather would often see his breath as, shivering, he raced and nimbly huddled under the shower's spray in the dead of winter. My father left no frugal stone unturned. For the shower stall, he laid a shallow concrete basin and finished it off by hanging a modest plastic curtain. To ensure no one would run up the water bill by taking long, reflective pleasure washings, he bought a basic, non-adjusting showerhead that was one inch in diameter. This squirt-gun-sized nozzle emitted a stream wide enough to cover ten percent of the bather's body, thus requiring him to turn and twist to warm areas that quickly became frostbitten outside the warm arc of falling water. To a man such as my father, trained in the art of standing baths, a shower was a modern indulgence. He never used it. He preferred his daily washings done over the sink during the week and a quick shallow bath on Saturday evening.

. . .

Joe is and always was smarter than I am. It seemed he didn't have to study at all to get straight A's while I struggled to get C's. He had taken his baby status and soared with it. He was vibrant, funny, and the center of attention, while I felt painfully shy and awkward. In trying too hard at everything, I was nervous about failing at anything. Despite the disparity in our talents, we never became competitors. He was generous to a fault, a saint in the making who always remained my friend and ally. We didn't have to explain ourselves to each other. Being well-schooled in the art of non-communication by our father, Joe and I could sit for hours watching a football game, working side by side in the mink yard or working out a jigsaw puzzle and never talk. Ries men are silent folks with busy minds.

My earliest years went along well enough until my first

year in kindergarten when I developed a painful stutter, a condition that prompted the school counselor to recommend I be held back a year to repeat kindergarten. The decision to hold a child back is a difficult one for a parent. In my case, it was all the more so because it would mean I'd go through school in the same grade as Joe. His name would be called right after mine during roll call. Worse still, the stigma of being the dumb brother would be stamped on my forehead.

As my stutter worsened, my parents began to think I might be learning disabled. More than likely, I had some form of Attention Deficit Disorder, but in the mid-1950s the idea of labeling hyperactive children mental misfits was unheard of. People just accepted that some kids, most often boys, were a little more rambunctious than others. In my case, it was not so much that I talked incessantly or raced about, it was that my tongue got tied. I'd be flooded with ideas and an urgency to express them, and inevitably I would begin to stutter. My brain would overload. I was a type-A personality whose mouth wasn't big enough for his mind.

My tongue stumbled on only a few words—*I, the, we* and *me.* I couldn't complete a sentence without hitting one of these four landmines. "Mom, can I-I-I go to th-th-th-the playground?" or "Mom, come with m-m-m-me, w-w-we have to read that book," or "I-I-I have to go to th-th-the bathroom I-I-I-I really do!" I was eager, earnest, and overflowing with inner words wanting to get out, but they all got log-jammed behind my front teeth. "Slow down, and think about what you are going to say," my mother would implore of her stammering young son. I would take a deep breath, close my eyes, and start over again, usually pausing between each word until I got all five or six of them out ten minutes later. My mother was patient but concerned.

My parents thought my speech impediment might be due to the thin band of tissue that lies under the tongue, called the frenulum, being too tight. They decided to take me to our family doctor to have a procedure called a frenectomy performed. The procedure would snip the frenulum, making my tongue longer, more flexible, and give me the capability to speak with the ease of Ricardo Montalban or Sir Alec Guinness. "Chucky, we've decided to have that little floppy skin thing under your tongue snipped. Maybe that will let your tongue move so you can talk normal," my mom said.

Normal? I thought I was normal? Everyone seemed intent on making me more normal. I began to reconsider myself in light of this new information. Maybe I wasn't normal enough? I could feel the priesthood slipping through my rosary-beaded fingers. I intensified my prayers. But even at five years old, I could see the vision of my service to the Lord evaporating before my eyes.

My parents felt such pity for me that they both came to the doctor's office with me. We entered the small waiting room, and I took a seat between them and tried to make sense of it all. I began to mutter to myself "Maybe if I-I-I-I just slowed down w-w-w-we could keep my tongue th-th-th-the way it is. I-I-I-I-I mean what's wrong with m-m-m-my tongue. I-I-I-I talk pretty good. Don't I-I-I-I-I?" I looked up at my mom, imploring her affirmative answer.

"There is nothing wrong with you or your tongue. You're a very smart, talented little boy. We just think maybe that little floppy skin thing under your tongue might be keeping you from talking normal." There it was again—that word.

I began to pray silently as I had been taught to do. I asked that the suffering I was about to endure make me a normal person. *Dear God, make this snip remove the marbles in my mouth. Please make me speak like a normal person. I'll never spit or bite Joe again. I'll stop breathing excessively on the back of his neck before we go to sleep at night just to piss him off and I won't envy his successes. Rather, I'll accept myself and my failings as gifts of your divine and perfect love,* I prayed as we waited for the doctor to call us into his office.

"Hello, Carl and Helen, how are you doing today?" the doctor greeted them as he came out of his office. "So, are we ready?" he asked.

Dr. Wagner was our family witch doctor. Short, stocky, with crew cut hair and grandma Moses glasses. He wore a white smock with his name embroidered on the front. His breath had the distinct odor of fresh mouthwash, which I assumed was the mandatory rinse he performed before getting up-close-and-personal with clients.

"You bet we're ready. Ready, willing, and able, aren't we, Chucky?" my mom said, giving me a small supportive hug.

Our procession meandered its way into Dr. Wagner's office. "Hey, there little guy. How're you today?"

"I-I-I-I'm fine. Th-th-there is nothing wrong with m-m-me. As y-y-you can see." I smiled bravely.

"Well, of course there's nothing wrong with you. You can relax because this isn't going to hurt at all. I'm just going to snip the skin under your tongue. Just a quick little snip with this scissors here." He held up the instrument that was going to make me normal—a pair of shiny chrome scissors. "It'll bleed a little bit, but it won't hurt that bad. Just stand tall, open your mouth wide and close your eyes."

I did as I was told. He grabbed my tongue, using some bandage gauze to get a firm hold in case it attempted a full-scale retreat back into my mouth. Pulling it forward and up, he proceeded to snip a half inch into the membrane. It hurt. A few tears welled up in my eyes, but I didn't cry. "Nice work, Chucky. You're a tough little fella. Didn't even cry. Here, put this ball of cotton under your tongue. It'll absorb the blood. You better not talk for a while. It's going to hurt if you do. But you're healthy enough to have a lollipop for being so brave." With that, he gave my parents a nod and sent us on our way.

As I sat in the back seat of our car, the area snipped by Dr. Wagner burned beneath my tongue, but I was sure that God had answered my prayer and the little suffering I was enduring was just about to set me free.

A few hours after getting home, my mom found me playing outside and asked, "How are you feeling? Do you want to try talking a little? See how it feels to have a tongue that's the right length?" I nodded my head vigorously in the affirmative. "Well, then, say something," she said. "Take your time. Think about what you're going to say and then say it."

I thought for a moment, gathered my forces of concentration, and said, "W-w-w-we d-d-d-id it! I-I-I-I can talk normal, ca-ca-can't I-I-I-I...?" I froze in confusion, panic, and defeat. God had not answered my prayer. Worse, my stumbling had spread to new words. The procedure had made me less normal. My fate was sealed. I was sentenced to one more year in kindergarten and I realized what the DIS in disabled meant—Dumb Idiotic Stutterer.

. . .

Midway though my second tour of duty in kindergarten, the public school system eliminated the preschool program at Wilson Elementary School and moved it to Jefferson Elementary a few blocks away. My mother shared the news with me, informing me that Joe and I were going to a new school for the final few months of kindergarten. I didn't want to go. I hated change. I didn't want to give up the sweet, kind Ms. Evelyn Welch, the teacher with the biggest lips I'd ever seen. Her cream-colored skin, raven black hair and those knockout lips, which were always a lustrous ruby red, mesmerized me. She was better looking than Rita Hayworth. She understood me. I raised my hand to answer every single question—even the ones I didn't know. "Think first about what you're going to say, Chucky, and then speak slowly and clearly. You're such a smart young man, I'm sure you'll give me the right answer," she sweetly cautioned. She thought I was special despite my speaking challenge. She let me clean the erasers, run errands, and otherwise hang out at her desk, gazing into her Mediterranean blue eyes and at that great set of lip smackers. We were a match made in heaven. Yet I was to be torn away from her and sent to a new school. None of this troubled my brother, who possessed a remarkable degree of self-confidence and adapted as life changed around him.

It was a cloudy day in March when my mom escorted Joe and me through the front door of Jefferson Elementary and led us to the two preschool classrooms. Jefferson was built in the thirties. It looked like a dark castle and smelled like old socks. As my mother walked with us down its wide corridors, I knew my life had taken a turn for the worse. As usual, my brother dove headfirst into this new world, making best friends almost as soon as he stepped foot into his classroom. After a short stop to deposit Joe, my mother walked me to my classroom, where Mrs. Marlene Ratkowski greeted us.

"Hello, Mrs. Ries, I'm Mrs. Marlene Ratkowski. I'm the head preschool teacher here at Jefferson. This must be your son, Chucky," she said in a quick, cheerful burst. "He'll love it here. Lots to learn, lots to do, and lots of fun too." But I could see through her. The pleasant, overblown welcome she'd performed for my mother didn't fool me; she was a monster whose job it was to crush the joy-filled little person in me. She was neither pretty nor sweet, and she certainly didn't have a set of mesmerizing lips like Ms. Welch. On the contrary, she had no lips at all. She was a large woman who wore her hair pinned up in a bun. I could smell fried food and mothballs as she gave me a welcoming hug. An organized woman of Polish descent, she ruled the room. She was there to break our spirits and teach us how to *behave*—sitting still, not talking, raising our hands before we spoke, and keeping our eyes glued on *her*.

"I wa-wa-want m-m-my Ms. Welch ba-ba-back. I-I-I do-do-don't want to b-b-b-be here. This is a big m-m-mistake," I said, snapping from fear and running for the door. I sprinted down the hall with Ratkowski in hot pursuit. She moved remarkably fast for a big woman. She matched my every twist and turn with one of her own. She'd obviously run down a few other free spirits in her day and was well conditioned. My legs were no match for her full sized pedal pushers, and she finally succeeded in grabbing my shirt collar from behind just as I reached the front door of the school and the prospect of freedom.

The commotion of our sprint down the hall produced a line-up of inquisitive heads poking out from every classroom up and down the preschool corridor. As I was marched back to my cell, I passed Joe. "Chuck, it'll be okay. You'll have fun once you get used to school. School is good for you," he said. What a guy. They didn't come any better. Rather than ridiculing me for being such a dipshit, he was telling me to buck up. He knew I could get on top of what I was feeling. But to me it was all wrong, and as my world collapsed, my bladder failed and everyone saw that the new boy had just lost it.

As we reentered the room, Mrs. Ratkowski said, a little out of breath, "Mrs. Ries, your son can really run. It looks like he's had a little accident though, haven't we, Chucky?"

I didn't reply, and, while she pitied me, my mother wasn't about to let wet pants get me a free day at home. "I'm so sorry. He gets a bit nervous at times. He doesn't do so well with changes. I'll just run home and get him a fresh pair of pants and underwear. Chucky, everything will be fine in a few days. I'll be right back with some fresh clothes," my mother said.

"That's super fine, Mrs. Ries. Come along now, Chucky. Let's take a tour of your new classroom and meet some of your classmates," Mrs. Ratkowski said. I shook the hands of my new classmates, many of whom I'd know for the rest of my life. Ratkowski's instruction was evident as her students chimed a warm "Good afternoon, Chuck. Welcome to preschool Room 109. We're so glad you could join us to prepare for a bright and successful future." I appreciated their kindness, but despite their excellent training, they could not conceal their curiosity about the stain of shame that stood before them.

The sunlit room and transcendent beauty of Ms. Welch had been replaced with a dungeon and a Polish dragon. I didn't need to worry about my stutter anymore because I'd never talk again.

· · ·

I survived my final three months of preschool. My stutter didn't get any better, but I did learn how to sit still, shut up, and only answer questions when I was called on. I ran out of Jefferson on the last day of school into a sunny early-June day, with robins singing and the wide-open spaces of summer vacation calling to me. Come September, I'd be a first grader at St. Peter Claver Elementary School, the school the Ries family helped build and continued to rule.

I faced my move to St. Peter Claver with the same fear and trembling I did every change. But I soon found that I wasn't the only idiot in first grade. I learned that out of the thirty-two boys in my first grade class, no fewer than ten had been held back in kindergarten, just like me. We were the slow learners. We were assigned to the Black Bird reading group, the Tortoise math circle, and the Three-Toed Sloth writing club. Maybe there was life after kindergarten, for here I found others like myself. Others who struggled to learn and talk and sit and raise their hands.

By fourth grade my stutter began to fade. I'd learned to slow down when I talked and carefully pronounce every word. At first my slow talking made people impatient as they waited for me to ask a question or give an answer. In fact, sometimes they didn't wait and would turn and walk away before I completed my perfectly enunciated reply. But my fellow Black Birds didn't care. I didn't have to fly like an eagle to be embraced by them. We got our hands dirty. We spoke with our bodies and with our actions, not with our mouths. To them I was normal.

4.

A Call to Cleanliness

"KIDS, it's bath time!!!" my mother called from downstairs.

My mother was pretty much a solo act when it came to parenting, and, but for a few child-rearing duties, my father was more than happy to stick to this arrangement. On the very short list of his domestic responsibilities was bathing his children. Bath time was already bad, given the often chilly, shallow conditions of our washing environment, but coupled with my father's underdeveloped abilities as provider of childcare, it was frightening. He came from the old school of bathing—scrub hard, do it fast, and get on with life. No soaking, no bubbles, and never raise the water level above six inches.

During the week I'd watch him perform his nightly bathing ritual. White strapper t-shirt, face towel in hand, bent over a sink full of warm water. He'd scrub his hands, arms, face, and armpits. He'd use the minimum amount of soap and water and rarely splash any of it out of the sink. I get more water on the bathroom floor brushing my teeth than he did during his standing baths. What he lacked in emotion he more than made up for in precision.

It was 6:30 p.m. on a Saturday evening in early December and those of us who had not yet left to begin our formal religious careers knew there was no escape. The call of our mother meant the five of us, ranging in age from two to nine years old, were headed for six inches of lukewarm water, chilly air, and damp towels, sitting shoulder to shoulder with our siblings. It was a unisex cleaning experience. My older sister, Sue, joined her four younger brothers until she was granted solo bathing status at age ten. We envied her. In our minds she'd escaped to a bathing spa replete with clear, fresh, warm water, dry towels, and solitude in which to let her young mind wander.

Our weekly bath began exactly at 6:30 p.m.. Dinner was over, the dishes were done, and it was one hour before the start of *The Lawrence Welk Show*. In sixty short minutes the show of shows would come beaming all the way from California into my father's home and castle in Sheboygan, Wisconsin. He knew there was only thing that stood between him and unadulterated viewing pleasure—his five dirty kids.

My father had few loves outside of church and work, but first among them was *The Lawrence Welk Show*. It was Lawrence Welk who popularized Champagne music. A musical genius from North Dakota whose minions included America's Sweethearts of Song, the Lennon Sisters; Myron Florin, the King of the Accordion; Ragtime Jo Ann Castle, the female melding of Liberace and Jerry Lee Lewis; and of course, Arthur Duncan, the black tap-dancing singer who thrilled us with his happy feet. Mr. Welk had assembled a crew of wholesome, smiling, God-love-America entertainers. My father also watched the Perry Como and Joey Bishop shows, but Lawrence Welk was a bird of another color. His great devotion to the show put it beyond the realm of possibility that he ever miss it.

The weekly bath wasn't so troubling in the spring, summer, or even early fall when weather in Wisconsin is kind to the young naked bather, but in November through

March, when winter winds blow and temperatures drop below freezing, bath time took on the worst aspects of the annual New Year's Day Polar Bear Club leap into Lake Michigan. The house temperature was kept low to save on heating oil. The water levels were kept low to save on the water bill. When it came to saving, my Depression-era parents knew no limits. I can't imagine, as I recall those forced marches to the bathtub, how we survived. My friends tell me, "Well, that's why you have so much character, that's why you're not just another mealy-mouthed, whiny-ass baby boomer." Maybe they're right, but must all triumphant character traits be forged out of misery? Can't character also be built in the warm, fragrant waters of a bubble bath?

Bathing was done in two shifts—the three older kids (Sue, John, and Jim) bathed first, followed by Joe and me. Those of us in the second squad knew and accepted the fate that awaited us—lukewarm water left over from the first group. Water that had a cloudy, soapy, mysterious look to it. Water that could contain secrets left behind.

The idea of recycling bath water didn't seem odd to my parents. To them it was just good common sense not to waste anything, even bath water. If three children could be cleaned in six inches of water, why not six or eight, or twenty for that matter? Water is water. We called it the bathing puddle.

Joe and I had none of the exotic comforts of our elder siblings. For us it was the double curse, no hot water and no dry towel. When our turn came we plucked up our courage, stripped, and tried to survive.

The process was simple. My father would scrub each of us with a face towel, following the exact same routine for each dirty bather. He'd run the towel up and down each arm, each leg, torso, face and bottom. He was quick and accurate. He didn't miss one dirty spot on any of his children. He'd conclude his hurried performance by showing his fun side and sculpt our shampoo-filled hair into a wild flip or wave. He'd then order us to raise our shivering bodies out of the water, and stand at attention so he could douse us with a pitcher of water drawn from the bathing puddle, telling us to "Close your eyes, here comes the water."

After the dousing, we'd jump out of the tub to be greeted by the same towel used to dry the three or four bathers who had preceded us. It was a moist sort of dry. In response to our protests for dry clean towels, my father would wisely proclaim, "Quiet, it's only damp. You've just had a bath. I washed you, scrubbed you, and you're all perfectly clean, and so is the towel. Why, when I was your age, back in the Middle Ages before they invented electricity, lights, and soap, we only took a bath once a year and we didn't complain." We were too cold to argue with his recollection of his childhood and hastily damped ourselves dry, slipped into our pajamas, robes, and slippers.

5.

The Big Two

ON SUNDAYS we would finish lunch around 1:00 p.m. and lay low until returning to the mink yard to do the second watering and feeding of the day. It was mid-July and over the summer I had worked hard to become a decent hardball player. I joined a Pee Wee League team. My mother got me clearance to leave farm work behind for the weekly game and occasional practice. I was bad. I didn't catch many pitches. The home plate umpire caught more than I did. But it wasn't completely because I lacked talent. In those days the catcher's mitts were microscopic and most Pee Wee League pitchers never threw strikes—at least ours didn't. So I was left to my own devices and did the best I could. My father was remotely aware that I had an interest in baseball, and on this day he decided to forsake his usual midday nap and invite me to play catch with him.

"Chucky, let's go play some catch."

"What?"

"Catch. Let's go play some catch in the barnyard."

"With who?"

"With me. Play catch with me."

"You and who else?"

"Just me. Play catch with me."

He must have thought I was hearing impaired, but his invitation for one-on-one fun came to my ears in a strange foreign language. I saw his lips move, but these were not the words that came out of them. I was used to no words coming from those lips, and when they did, they never offered fun.

My mother, who was standing nearby as he spoke, recognized my confusion and quickly stepped in to interpret. "Chucky, your dad wants to play catch with you." She enunciated each word. "He even has a baseball glove with him. Why don't *you* go play catch with *your* dad?" My mother's words broke through my bewilderment, and, while I didn't completely trust or understand what was being said to me, I agreed to play catch with my father.

My grandparents' faded red barn was three stories high. It was made of simple lumber and covered with sheet metal. Long before I was born, my grandfather added an extension to it that was the same size as the original structure. The addition, when it was attached to the existing building, created an "L". The inner joint of this elbow was called The Barnyard. It was here that we had an old-fashioned manual water pump, a small chicken coop, and a flatbed wagon once used for farm work, onto which we tossed biodegradable waste from hundreds of meals we had each month. We called it the garbage wagon and once it was full, we attached it to our tractor and towed it below the mink yard to be dumped. The grass in the barnyard was cut short and was turning brown from the heat and lack of rain, and, as always, flies buzzed in abundance.

My father wore his usual Oshkosh B'Gosh gray-and-blue striped bib overalls and his National Mink Foods baseball cap with the likeness of our favorite furred animal embroidered on the front. As we took our throwing positions, he looked nothing like a baseball player, but what did it matter? If *that* man was my father and he was about to play catch with me, who was I to say what a baseball player did or did not look like?

For twenty minutes farm-father and farm-son silently tossed the baseball around the barnyard. The farm-father wasn't too bad. In fact, he was better than his goofy-looking baseball outfit might at first suggest. Somewhere in a past I did not know, this man had thrown a baseball before. Before the mink and before the kids, he had taken time to actually throw a baseball. I was impressed and hopeful. The endless repetition of throw and catch felt natural and ordained. We were living a moment shared by millions of other fathers and sons. I could feel my heart drawing toward him as I hurled the ball back, trying to impress him. Trying to show him that his kid had the right stuff.

"Well, time to get back to work," he said, killing the moment before it had a chance to grow. I sensed he was relieved to return to gainful activity. *Catch* was an abstraction serving no productive end. Somewhere in the recesses of his mind, he felt it was a good thing to do—to play catch with one's son—but his genetic code told him that *character* was not built by playing baseball. Character is built during hard work and Godly service. I stood back as he walked away, holding the ball and waiting for him to turn around. But he didn't turn and we never played catch again.

He never came to any of my ball games. My team went 0–11 for the season. After that summer, I gave up trying to be a reasonably good baseball player. I never connected my failure with my father. At nine years of age you don't make those connections. You take the cards you're dealt, and nothing about these cards was weird or surprising. They were just what they were. I'd notice other parents at my games. I figured they were people who didn't have to work for a living. The lack of attention my father paid me was life as usual. Besides, my father's favorite sport wasn't baseball, it was work.

. . .

The cranberry swamp was just below our farm. It was usually filled with low-lying water and an abundance of cattails. Black birds lived and nested there as well as countless rabbits. It was five acres in diameter with a murky pool at the center where muskrats built their hutches. In the dead of winter we'd go ice skating there, swerving and weaving our way in and out of the cattails and around the muskrat hutches. At the north end of the swamp was a small wooded area filled with box elder saplings. My father called them weeds of the forest because they grew fast and in just about any condition, including those of a swamp.

We never walked in the swamp until it froze over in early winter. But this autumn, after a particularly dry summer, we found ourselves being able to run through it and play hide-and-seek in it. My eleven cousins, who lived nearby, and my siblings would play war by pulling off the tops of cattails and using them to beat each other over the head, sending plumes of cottony seedlings into the air. It was a natural playground with unending things to see and experience.

Pheasant hunting season began in late fall. Most of the cornfields had been harvested by this time, and the birds were fat from dining under apple and cherry trees, and eating corn dropped by the combines. It was one brilliant, clear day in autumn. The sky was bright blue and the landscape burst with fall colors. It was late Saturday afternoon. The second round of chores were over, and, as I was walked through the feed house, I found my father loading his twenty-two rifle.

"Let's go hunting," he said, looking up at me.

"What?"

"Hunting, in the swamp. I set up a blind. Let's get some pheasants."

My older siblings had already gone into the house for the day—it would just be the two of us.

My father and I walked to the bottom of the mink

yard, hopped the guard fence, and walked another one hundred yards through towering cattails toward the center of the swamp. The ground was uncharacteristically firm and easily held both of us. My father had come down earlier in the week and piled a few old, wooden fence posts into an informal barrier for us to hide behind. Along with his rifle, he'd brought a burlap bag filled with cobs of dry seed corn. As he settled in behind the blind, he told me, "Take this and dump it about two hundred feet up ahead. Just dump it in one big pile and get back here. We'll see who's hungry today." I did as he told me and ran back with the empty burlap bag flying behind me, jumping over the blind and settling in beside him. "Don't talk, don't move, just watch the corn pile," he said.

We lay on our bellies and watched the center of the swamp bed where he had told me to place the corn. His rifle rested on one of the posts, and we waited for the birds to find the corn. I never got this physically close to my father. I don't remember him ever hugging me or directly talking to me other than to give me reprimands or directions about work. But on this sun-drenched afternoon in the heart of the cranberry swamp, I lay perfectly still and soaked in the odor of his work clothes. I listened to the slow, steady rhythm of his breathing and

inhaled the aroma of his Blue Boar pipe tobacco, argu-
ably the worst smelling pipe tobacco ever created.

The air was dry and warm. The cattails swayed to a
breeze that blew out of the southwest. The familiar, low
hum of insects had slowly lulled me into sleep when
the *crack* of my dad's rifle shook me awake. "Got him!
Hustle out there and grab it," my father ordered in a loud
whisper.

My father's twenty-two was precise and quiet. With
a scope mounted on its barrel, it was deadly accurate.
Unlike a twelve-gauge shotgun that blew birdshot, the
twenty-two shot small bullets. Because of its relative
silence, it didn't scatter other birds that might be hiding
nearby. Rather, they'd sit tight and, once the coast was
clear, begin to move and return the pile of corn.

I ran out, grabbed the bird, and hustled back to the
blind, placing it between my father and me as we resumed
our vigil. This time I kept my eyes open. In about fifteen
minutes a few more birds appeared, circling the corn pile
and feeding. My father took aim at the rooster with its
distinctive red-ringed neck and nailed him, again telling
me to run and get it. We recommenced our waiting and
my father soon laid out his third bird for the afternoon.
By the end of our two hours together, we'd bagged three

hens and two roosters with five clean shots. "That'll do it. That's pretty damn good. We're going to be eating some pheasant. Let's head back before your mom thinks we got lost."

We worked our way back through the cattails. I walked behind, carrying the five birds in the burlap bag while my father carried his rifle. We hopped back over the guard fence and walked to the carpenter shop where my father quickly and efficiently cleaned the birds. We then went into the house for dinner.

At the kitchen table that evening, my father, true to form, didn't say much about our time together other than, "It went well. We were lucky to get five birds," before returning to his meal.

Knowing she wasn't going to get much information from him, my mother turned to me and asked, "Well, did you have fun with your dad, Chucky? What was it like hunting for pheasants? Was it exciting?"

Like my father, I was taciturn in my reply and gave my mother a minimum of, "Yup, I had fun, Mom; we got five birds." I had to fight myself to keep from saying more. I wanted to shout and tell everyone how great it was to be with my father, to lie next to him in a pheasant blind, and how proud I was to be his son. I wanted to tell them what a perfect day it had been and that I wanted one hundred more just like it, but I knew that if I did I would break the spell and I would lose him forever. I wanted to tell them I was afraid he'd evaporate like mist in the morning sun if I adored him too much. So there at the dinner table, I became nothing. I didn't express my excitement or publicly adore my father. I tried to be silent, stoic, and numb. Like him, I ate with my head down and shoved my feelings to the floor. I strangled the ball of joy that was rising up in me. I chewed my food and concentrated on becoming like him, because I knew that if I could become like him it would bring me more days like today.

6.

Fish Creek

MY FATHER was forty-five years old when I was born. He had lived half his life when I arrived. I sometimes look at pictures of him as a young man and try to know him. I try to reach into the silence that surrounded him like a still, lifeless cloud and see into his true nature. I see him playing cards with friends, steins of beer on the card table, holding a big cigar with a 1940 Ford in the background. I see him dressed elegantly in a dark suit before a rugged fieldstone wall holding a straw fedora hat in his hand or leaning against a log fence wearing a wool plaid hunting jacket and knee-high, laced hiking boots. I see a handsome man, five feet nine inches tall, one hundred and seventy pounds, built lean and strong, with black hair, green eyes, and a full smile that is measured and steady. When I look at these pictures, I know the man I grew up with was not always made of vapor. I know he laughed, had passions and pleasures. I stare and I listen and I become perplexed that I cannot match my experience of him with those images. But maybe this is how it's meant to be. Maybe children never know their parents. Perhaps, like so much of what enters our lives, we experience them through our own unique filters. Maybe we never *see* them at all.

My father chose not to follow his grandfather and become a dairy farmer. After graduation from eighth grade, he worked on his father's farm and then tried being a sheet metal worker, but he'd always wanted to work for himself. Since a friend of his was having some success at raising mink, he thought he would give it a try. He uncharacteristically invested his entire life savings of one thousand dollars and bought breeding stock. Over a forty-year career he earned the reputation of having the finest mink in the country.

My father was a man of few words, yet his beliefs were deeply held. I often wondered why he hadn't become a priest himself; he clearly loved God more than parenting. Just as he overachieved in piety and work, he was equally impressive when it came to silence. Its brilliance was never more evident than during the dinner hour when the chattering and reaching of his children collided with him at the table in our too-small kitchen. It was typical family pandemonium—milk glasses spilling, forks and knives clinking, and one or another sibling kicking the other under the table, all punctuated by screams of protest. My mother's prayerful refrain was, "Carl, say something!"

It was at this moment in the proceedings that we'd raise our collective heads, still our busy hands, silence our mouths, and turn in unison to face the man at the head of the table—*Our Father*. Each night we'd wait to see if he would say or do something to help our mother who was racing like a short order cook during rush hour, but the miracle that we all felt was right and just never came. My father would say what he said every night of every day during the thousand dinners we shared, "Well, what do you want me to say?" That was it—Well, *what do you want me to say?* We could have sung those words along with him, so certain were we that they'd be the answer to my mother's cry for help.

My father's obliviousness might have prompted a more modern woman to say something. Make her try to break through the thick headedness of her husband's male nature, but not my mother. She'd never complain or shout. She was the perfect team player even though it meant she had to play every position. She didn't lack backbone. She'd shoot my father a look that could vaporize a legion of barbarians, but to her long-suffering, Christian Mother credit, she never mentioned her irritations with him until after he had passed away. She carried his cross and made him a better man and gave heart to our family.

. . .

Outside of church and work, my father found his greatest comfort in nature. It had been his dream to become a forest ranger, but the cost of schooling would prevent this. While he permitted himself precious little time for recreation, he occasionally found time for a hike. His preferred destination was Fish Creek.

Fish Creek was a tiny finger of water that meandered its way toward the Sheboygan River and on into Lake Michigan. Most months it barely moved, crawling through a series of low, rolling farm fields on the eastern the edge of the Kettle Moraine Forest. I was ten years old when I began to walk its length, stopping to explore a curious hole in the bank, or inspect tracks left behind by a muskrat, raccoon, deer, or fox. I'd sit on its modest banks under looming willow trees and stare into the water and out into space. It was my place.

After a series of heavy spring rains, I grabbed two of the trident-tipped broom handles my father had jury-rigged for sucker fishing. These bottom-feeding lake fish would run upstream to spawn when the creek was high and the water was fresh and clean. I'd finished my chores, grabbed a peanut butter sandwich and baling twine, and headed out across the familiar fields, county trunk roads, and occasional swamp that led me to Fish Creek. One of the fields I crossed belonged to my father's boyhood friend, Roland Gimble. He too owned a mink farm. It was warm for May. The sun hid behind gray rain clouds as I walked along a route I knew with my eyes closed.

"Well, if it isn't a Ries boy. What you up to, Chucky?" I heard a familiar voice shout to me a short distance away. "How come you ain't working? If your dad can't find work for you, maybe I can?" I turned and saw Roland Gimble fixing the guard fence that surrounded his mink yard.

"I'm going spear fishing. My chores are all done," I said.

"Well, you better be damn sure you don't fall in that creek. Cold walk home if you do. I hear they saw some sharks coming up to spawn this year. Big ones too! Ten feet long and teeth so big, white, and shiny you can see your reflection in them right before they chomp down and eat you. I'd be darn careful if I was you. You watch that little behinder of yours or you'll be a shark sandwich."

"I won't fall in. I know better than that. And I'll keep my eyes open for sharks. Maybe I'll spear one!" I said as I waved and walked on by. He looked up again, winked his approval, and went on with his work.

When I arrived at Fish Creek, I began to poke my spear under the edge of the banks and look for shadows in the water, just as my father's hired man, Marvin Rammer, had shown me a few weeks earlier. Marvin would be the only help my father would ever use other than his own children. Marvin found his God in living, with the same passion that my father found his God in church. If we'd finish farm chores early and the weather was right, he'd invite a Ries boy or two to join him on a quick, late afternoon trip down to the creek. Usually it was one of my older brothers, Jim or John, who would join him.

Marvin was six feet tall, broad-shouldered, and built like a bull. His brown eyes, tanned skin, and full head of dark hair, made him to mink farms what Errol Flynn must have been to pirate ships. He had so much sex appeal and charm, he could have been in the movies. There seemed to be nothing about life he didn't know and didn't want to share. He whistled while he worked and always had a wisecrack or words of wisdom to share. We flocked to him like life-starved rats to a pied piper. After working on my father's ranch, he would often enlist Jim and John to join him in baling hay for area farmers and doing odd jobs as his low-paid lackeys. He'd take them fishing, deer hunting, duck hunting, horseback riding, snowmobiling, and rough housing. He taught us how to work hard with utter joy. He explained the complexities of sex and how to drink beer. My parents' prayers had produced a second miracle equal to the vocations of their children—Marvin Rammer.

Marvin had told me that suckers love to hide in the small nooks and crannies along the banks of the creek. They liked to face upstream along small rapids and let the oxygen-rich water speed through their gills. As I kicked a few loose from under the bank, I lunged back and forth over the narrow band of water, chasing them until I landed two in quick succession with my spear. I let the spear fly as often as I could. I didn't care if I hit or missed.

After a few hectic hours, I'd caught a string of six

good-sized suckers. It had been an excellent day. With my shoes wet and caked with mud and my pants soaked from the waist down, I proudly walked the two miles back home. I smelled of fish and creek. As I passed the Gimble Ranch, Rollie was still outside fixing his guard fence. "See any sharks out there today, Chucky? Looks like you still got both your legs attached and that little behinder of yours ain't missing. You're a smart kid; I didn't think you'd let those sharks eat you for lunch."

"Nope, no sharks got me today, but I got six suckers," I replied and held up my baling twine heavy with fish, showing him the trophies.

"I see that. Looks like you were smarter than those fish today."

"Yup, I think you're right," and I continued on my way home.

. . .

The next day I was working with Jim, Marvin, and my dad doing the afternoon feeding. Jim and I were required to walk ahead of my father and Marvin, and open and close the feed trays, on which they placed the high-protein slop mink thrived on. Using industrial-sized metal spoons, they scooped feed out of a three-gallon bucket carried waist high and held in place with a wide leather strap slung over the shoulder. Feeding took an hour and included a fair amount of stupid banter between Marvin and the boys. My father occasionally jumped in with a word or two, but mostly preferred to listen and enjoy the entertainment.

A few days earlier Jim had gone sucker fishing with Marvin and a few of his buddies. He was eager to relive the experience and, as always, make it bigger than it actually was.

. . .

Jim had a natural gift for gab. He was the entertainment ambassador my mother would send out of the kitchen and into the living room when my parents had guests over for dinner. He'd regale them with a variety of badly told jokes, magic tricks, and oddball monologues while my mom made drinks or prepared snacks in the kitchen. The wise woman knew my father had only five minutes of good dinner party patter in him. So after my father had run out of things to say and the uneasy silence began to descend on the festivities, Jim would bound into the center of the room, and with crew cut, freckles, and buckteeth, would become the cocktail hour entertainment. In fact, he was so good, that he was often given dimes and nickels from the appreciative guests.

Besides a gift for gab, Jim could also dissemble the truth to suit his own purposes. In fact, he could turn anything into the truth. Little white lies became kernels of wisdom as they were processed through his quick and fertile mind.

I remember one such valiant performance when it looked as if *The Lawrence Welk Show* was going to win out over a TV movie we had all been looking forward to seeing. "Mom, the show starts in two minutes. You know, the one about the spaceship and the alien walking out of it? They blow up the capitol. People run all over the place, screaming, and die. The *TV Guide* calls *The Day the Earth Stood Still* the best science fiction movie ever made. We didn't mind putting off *The Sound of Music* or *Doctor Zhivago* a few weeks ago so dad could get his polka fix, but this is different. This is very different!" he pleaded, pausing to catch his breath and wipe a few tears of pure fabrication from his eyes. Even we, his four siblings who had witnessed other performances, were pretty impressed by his efforts. He was giving it all away. Leaving every ounce of bullshit in him on the playing field.

Where does he come up with this stuff? we wondered, looking on with pride at our brother. If anyone could make my mother realize that our happiness was more important than another thirty minutes of the maestro from North Dakota, it was Jim. We pushed him a few feet closer toward our mother and cleared a space for him to let his imagination take wing. His task was great, for he was up against my father, the undisputed king of NO. We often thought it was the only word my father knew. He knew it in five different languages. It rolled off his tongue like a monument to appropriate parenting. If anyone could get him to bend and allow us to cut in on his hour of pure happiness, it would be my mother, and it would be Jim's eloquent appeal that would make her do it.

"Mom, I have been asked by my three brothers and sister now standing around me to beg your intervention with our father. We know he loves watching *that* show. You do, however, understand that a flying saucer is about to land on earth and threaten our very existence? The people of earth are counting on us!" It was desperation time. Jim signaled for us to hit the floor. We fell to knees and assumed the prayer position we had perfected during daily mass, too many rosaries, and way too many religion classes. Our eyes gazed up at our mother, our Madonna, and Jim completed his performance with a bold and very impressive, "You have to do something! Can't you see how important this is to us? We don't ask for much. We usually suffer in silence. We eat leftovers and wear patched clothing, but, Mom, you must do something!" He tried to make her realize that disappointments such as this would leave deep psychological scars in a child. Scars that would fester until one horrible day that very child snaps, robs a bank, and while being led away to jail before a national television audience says, "If my mother had let me watch *The Day The Earth Stood Still*, this would never have happened. Please, all you parents out there, if you have children of your own and you love them, let them watch whatever TV show they want. Do it now. Do it before it's too late!"

Jim rounded out his performance with a simple and direct, "If you really love us, you will come to our rescue. You will look into our young beating hearts and realize that the future of this great land is hanging in the balance," and then he stopped, maintaining radio silence for fifteen seconds as he gazed up at my mother, certain of his victory. Jim's oratory and our choreographed supplication delighted my mother. But sadly and with great regret, she had to acknowledge what we feared.

"Kids, it's your dad's favorite show. He works hard all week. He deserves to watch Lawrence Welk." She pitied us, that much was clear. But she too was no match for my father's "NO", his immovable, immutable mantra, and she knew better than to apply any pressure to him. But that didn't mean she couldn't bribe her children. "How about if I make you all a root beer float? That would be special, right? A root beer float is a lot better than a flying saucer." She was doing her best under extremely desperate circumstances. Her offer had weakened our resolve. We would swallow our pride and surrender to Lawrence Welk, but only if she'd throw in chips with the root beer float. Watching us in our kneeling positions, she agreed. "Root beer floats and potato chips it is. You can all get up off your knees now," she smiled, impressed with the unanimity of our negotiating effort and a little concerned with Jim's growing ability to let his mouth exceed the confines of reality.

. . .

As Jim walked ahead of my father and opened feeders, he proclaimed, with his characteristic embellishments, "Man, did I score! Did I hit it big! I must have taken thirty shots. The stream was so full of suckers, I could have walked across it on their scaly backs. I should have come home with twenty on my stringer. Ain't that right, Marv?"

"You betcha, Jimmy. You're a sucker fisherman, that's for sure. But I'm not sure if it's your technique or just your good looks. Those fish couldn't take their eyes off you. You should've seen it, Carl; they practically jumped into his pocket. I've never seen anything like it in my whole life. Why, with the sun reflecting off his two buck teeth, those poor fish were blinded like deer in head-lights. Yes, sir, that boy's a sucker's best friend," Marvin replied from three rows over as he and I worked our way down another row of mink.

"You bet I'm a sucker's best friend and you're jealous you're not. I landed a boatload and you only got those two scrawny, little bitsy minnows. What are you going to do with them, put them in a fish bowl until they grow up? I thought it was against the law to take two-inchers? Good thing the game warden didn't come along. How hard up can you get, stringing baby fish? And one more thing while I think of it," Jim continued, as he was physically unable to keep one word that passed through his mind from coming out of his mouth. "You're so ugly, you scared the fish to death, and what's more, you sort of look like a fish and you smell like one too, pee-ew," Jim roared with pleasure.

Marvin and I kept working our way down our aisle as my dad and Jim worked theirs. "Well, Chucky got six suckers yesterday and they were good-sized. How many did you get, Jimmy?" my dad asked.

"Well, heck, I got eight regular suckers and five really huge cocksuckers. Right, Marvin? Didn't I get some big cocksuckers?" Jim asked.

Marvin's eyes opened wide and he squeezed his mouth shut to keep from exploding with laughter. As always, Jim was in the ballpark, but off in left field. For indeed he did get thirteen suckers that day, but none of them were of the variety he mentioned. Jim's ears were as big as his mouth and just as prone to confusing the truth. He'd heard the words, but misunderstood what they meant each time Marvin's spear had missed its target and he'd yelled, "Why, that little cocksucker!"

Hearing Jim's misunderstanding, Marvin hastily kneeled down to tie his shoe and get out of my father's line of sight. He gave Marvin the same look he always did when one of his sons said or did something they could have only learned from one person. But he never said anything about it. Moments like these seemed to overload my father's circuits and leave the quiet man speechless.

Not being a complete idiot, Jim sensed something was awry and after a moment of reflection shouted over to Marvin, who was having difficulty tying his shoe, "Well, Marvin, isn't that right? Didn't I nail those cocksuckers right through their fish brains?"

Realizing that silence was a virtue as well as the better part of valor, Marvin decided to let this line of conversation die. After a few moments of silence, Jim's mouth, knowing no limits, rambled on to other things. But he managed to figure out that cocksuckers were not a species of fish.

7.

I Dare You

UNDER the canopy of the great oak tree and in the grove of crab apple trees, my grandparents held the annual Ries Summer Picnic. It was the unofficial end-of-summer celebration. Family and friends from throughout Sheboygan County were invited. They arrived in mid-afternoon and stayed late into the night.

Preparing food for this party was an act of love—a physical way of showing affection in a family where hugs and kisses were seldom exchanged. The more food you made, the greater your embrace. My uncles huddled around the grills, drinking beer from an iced keg, turning the chickens, hamburgers, sausages, and sweet corn. My aunts gathered in the kitchen, chopping, stirring, and taking orders from my grandmother.

My grandmother began her preparation weeks in advance. Like most German farm wives born in the mid-1800's, she understood the exacting logistics and planning required to feed over one hundred people. No detail was too small to escape her well-trained eye. Secretly, I think her motive for creating this spectacle was not only the love of her family, but also the hidden desire to rule supreme. She was, after all, Queen of the Ries Clan and it was her job to keep a watchful eye so as to maintain order within her domain. I pitied her two daughters, my aunts Iris and Alice. How could they ever measure up to a woman the stature of my grandmother?

The afternoon before the picnic, my siblings and cousins helped my grandfather prepare for the party, pounding in the spikes for horseshoes, setting the nets for volleyball, and placing old doors on an army of sawhorses to serve as tabletops. They then covered the doors with red-and-white-checkered tablecloths, and topped them with vases of wild flowers. Since inexpensive folding chairs were a new invention in the late 1950s, the three families who lived within walking distance were asked to bring their kitchen chairs and place them around the tables. This picnic was much like all the rest. Only this year my cousin Allen managed to get his head stuck in the back of one of my grandmother's kitchen chairs.

Allen was the kind of kid who would take any dare. This unique quality almost made you hesitate to dare him at all. If you were foolish enough to suggest to Allen that he jump out of a tree, or steal a handful of jawbreakers at Shirtzel's Five & Dime, Allen would jump out of the tree and steal the jawbreakers. If you dared him to ride his bike down the steepest hill in Sheboygan, where certain death lay waiting at the bottom, he'd descend at full speed without another word, peddling as if possessed by the devil for maximum speed and maximum impact. Whatever there was to look forward to at nine years old, you knew he'd already been there, and if he hadn't, he'd make up a big lie that was every bit as enjoyable as the truth. He was a man-boy. The rest of us were mere boy-boys, pretenders in the face of adventure.

Maybe he turned out to be such a terror because his mother, Aunt Iris, was so rigid and his father, Bernie, so beaten down. I can't remember Aunt Iris ever smiling. I can hardly remember Uncle Bernie at all. He was invisible in my aunt's large, dark shadow.

My aunts were born at a time when most women didn't have jobs or careers outside of raising their children. For Iris this was a pity. She could have run General Motors or the Fifth Armored Tank Division. Lacking such opportunities, she focused her mighty powers of concentration on making sure Allen was brought up right—no, perfect—no, destined to rule the world. Allen seemed to instinctively know this about his mother and relished opportunities to disrupt her well-laid plans.

Among Allen's physical attributes, one stood out among all others. He had an unusually large head. My family is full of large-headed people. Jim had the distinction of wearing the largest football helmet on his high school team, and my head is an ample size eight. But Allen's head was a rare beauty—big, red, and round, the perfect complement to his Pillsbury doughboy body.

During the picnic, my cousins and I, ranging in age from five to fourteen years old, wandered my grandparents' dairy farm like a band of gypsies. We'd go through our usual list of picnic pastimes. We'd play in the hayloft building forts out of hay bales. We'd prove to ourselves again that cats could swim by dropping those dumb enough to come near us into the cow trough. And having exhausted this repertoire, we turned our attention to less exciting fare—a rousing game called "Stick Your Head Through the Chair."

I am not sure why we singled out my grandparents' chairs for this exercise in Russian roulette. Maybe because they were the best of the bunch we had to choose from. They were made of sturdy oak, stained a shiny brown, and had strong doweled spindles running the length of their backs. Equally important was the fact that the spindles were spaced just far enough apart to allow the curious, the fearless, and the foolish to put their heads through—just to see if it could be done.

It was an easy game to play. You'd push your head through the five-inch gap between the rungs of the chair and pull it out again. The thrill was in the extraction and the possibility you might never get your head out again. This caused a lot of laughs and a few seconds of fear. With a little bit of tugging and a small amount of pain, all of us popped through the opening and out again. When it was Allen's turn, we warned him that he would never get his head through the narrow opening, and if he did, he would never get it back out again.

"Allen, don't do it. You'll never pull that big melon of yours out. You'll live the rest of your life with a chair wrapped around your head!" I warned him.

My cousin Pat, who lived next door, joined in, "Besides, your mom won't be very happy with you showing up at church tomorrow morning wearing one of Grandma's chairs wrapped around that big head of yours." We thought it was too funny and were certain that our cautionary pleas would never deter Allen.

When it was Allen's turn to thrust his head into danger, he did not hesitate. Stepping up to the chair, he mocked a Charles Atlas muscleman pose and assumed the bent position preferred by aficionados of this particular sport. It took a great deal of effort to push his head through the spindles, but in true Allen style, he managed to do it. We cheered. We clapped. We slapped him on the back. We exalted in his devil-may-care attitude.

If only I could be just a tiny bit like Cousin Allen, I silently thought. I was in awe of him. I could not imagine there would ever come a time when I would be as fearless as he.

"There, I did it! You're just a bunch of weenie babies," Allen said, his ears red. He was a bit out of breath from the exertion of his feat. "Why, I could have shoved it through an opening half as big. I'm like the Great Houdini." We all agreed and shouted our appreciation at his remarkable achievement.

After milking the moment, Allen turned his powers of concentration to removing his head. He pulled and pried, but to no avail. No matter what he did, he could not pull his head out of the chair. All the laughter and commotion soon attracted the attention of my grandfather and a few uncles who were working the grills nearby. They found Allen's feat equally worthy of admiration and enjoyed his predicament for a few minutes.

"Bernie, you have quite a kid there," Uncle Ray said as he topped off Uncle Bernie's beer. Bernie looked somewhat humiliated and defeated, but took the teasing in good humor and asked those assembled to help him get his son's head out of the chair.

Telling us to step back, my uncles inspected Allen like surgeons about to do a heart by-pass procedure. Slowly and carefully, they began the process of pulling the protruding object from the back of the chair. After fifteen minutes they gave up and sent one of us to fetch my grandmother.

Wearing her faded floral apron, she trundled over to the gawking circle of spectators and quickly surmised the problem. Uncle Ray suggested, "Ma, maybe we could just saw the spindle off the chair and get his head out? Won't take but a minute or two." But my grandmother would have none of it. It didn't matter how much Allen yelled or Aunt Iris demanded he be set free, she was not about to ruin her chair. My grandma would not be moved; her feet were as firmly rooted as the oak tree she stood under.

When her mind was made up, it did not change. She would not ruin her good chair. She would not get Allen's head out of the chair until she was ready.

As Grandma walked back into her kitchen, Aunt Iris again implored her to set her son free. "I'm too busy to get his head out. Besides, he's nothing but trouble, that boy. Little *dumkopf* (bonehead)! He deserves what he gets." My grandmother continued to growl in her thick accent as she sliced potatoes for German potato salad. Staring out the kitchen window, she continued, "Look at him, that little *scheister* (shit), entertaining everyone with his head stuck in my chair. That child is not right," she fumed, all the while slicing potato after potato with the precision and speed of a Samurai master.

My kind and soft-spoken grandfather tried to prevail upon his imposing wife, and, while sympathetic to Allen's plight, knew better than to proceed with any strategy to free his head until his wife gave her consent. So, heads bowed, all those assembled in the kitchen continued to slice potatoes and stir the many dishes being prepared for the crowd outside. No one was going to disrupt my grandmother's proudest day and especially not Allen.

The events of the day went on as planned and Allen was escorted to the porch where he would wait out his sentence. Moments like these would have been sheer embarrassment for me, but Allen turned them into opportunities to entertain and command an audience.

"Hey, Chucky! You ever hear the story about the couple who got chopped up by a one-armed axe murderer?" Allen asked.

"Hey, Pat! Did you see that vampire film where the guy gets all the blood sucked of out him?" he continued. He was a wonder of the world. He could not, would not, be brought down. His spirit was as big and indomitable as his large, hard head.

"Chucky, remember the time I ate three earthworms and washed 'em down with chocolate milk?" he shouted, laughing and snorting with self-pleasure.

Sitting on a milking stool my grandfather had brought for him, Allen sipped lemonade though a straw and regaled us with his stories. He was the King of Comedy. Even in adversity, he could draw a crowd.

A few hours passed. With the dishes washed, dessert set out, and continued gentle pleading by Grandfather, my grandmother finally decided to turn her attention to setting Allen free. Grandma had a plan.

As she approached, the crowd surrounding Allen parted like the Red Sea making way for Moses. In her small, sturdy hands, she carried a large, brown crockery pot. At first I was unsure why she'd bring such a thing with her from the kitchen, but then the brilliance of my grandmother's mind flooded over me—she had the fat-dripping jar.

Most rural families kept excess fat and grease from cooking in a crock-pot they stored under the kitchen sink. Rather than send grease and fat down the drain, they simply poured it into a crock-pot or bucket and disposed of it when full. I realized then that my grandmother was not going to use perfectly good cooking oil to liberate Allen. No, his fate was to be far fattier than that.

As my grandmother drew near, she said, "So, my little dumpling, it's time for Grandma to free you." I detected a slight shudder in Allen's heroic demeanor. As fearless and as brave as he was, he knew my grandmother was not a woman to be messed with.

"Oh, hi, Grandma Mary," his tone was syrupy. "What do you have in the jar? Are you going to get me out? Why, I hope it's not too much of a bother..."

"Just shut your mouth, close your eyes, and start pulling when I tell you to," she commanded. She reached into her crock-pot and pulled out a fistful of fat, grease, and remnants of past meals and began to rub it onto Allen's large head. She was like a Turkish masseuse gone mad. She worked with a diligence and thoroughness that would have made her German ancestors proud. I don't think she missed an inch of Allen's head and when she finished I saw what appeared to be a slight smile creep over her lips. My grandma, like most Germans from the hard, farm-life school of living, didn't smile a great deal. But, for just a moment, I saw the edges of her lips turn toward the sun as she bent over her special grandson and not-so-gently pushed his head with one hand and pulled the back of his shirt collar with the other. She pushed and she pulled. She would not be defeated. It didn't matter that one of Allen's ears might be sacrificed in the effort to free him. In a few moments his head popped free and my grandmother, making no to-do about it, returned to the kitchen and went back to her work. "There. Done. Good. Back to work," she said, as she trundled off to the kitchen.

Allen's head was thoroughly covered in fat remnants. Aunt Iris lost no time in marching him into the bathroom and scrubbing the grease from his head. We cheered our grandmother and gave Allen two thumbs-up as he waved to us before his mother yanked him into the house.

. . .

Unlike Allen, I did not come into the world with the balls of a bull. I was a dreamer, not a fighter. A lover, not a leaper. I read the lives of the saints while my friends read the lives of sports heroes. But because I had a large circle of cousins, I was often thrown into the circle of outrageous challenges and crazy leaps of faith. All the members of my tribe were empowered to throw down the gauntlet to adventure, but none stood taller than Allen did. He was the uncontested king of I Dare You.

"I Dare You" is the rite of passage all boys must pass on their journey to manhood. I've never heard these words floating above a group of girls, but for my fifth grade buddies and me, it was our mantra. It was our cry to a patriarchal God to turn our prepubescent bodies and minds into hard-hammered steel. No doubt some of these self-styled boy-gladiators were just a bunch of mindless hotheads, but an equal number seemed to be men from the time they jumped out of the womb. I was not one of them.

One Saturday afternoon a small band of us were riding our bikes aimlessly, as ten-year-old boys are prone to do. We'd done the pennies on the railroad tracks, gotten our shoes soaked in the Sheboygan River catching frogs, and sat through a softball game at Roosevelt Park. That's when it came to Allen that we should all ride our bikes down Kiwanis Park Hill. "Hey guys, I've got an idea. I have a huge idea!" he said as if God had just spoken to him. "I dare you to ride your bikes down Kiwanis Hill, from the high end. If that doesn't bust your nuts, I don't know what will," he said with the rush of adrenaline his brainchild had given him.

I agreed it would indeed bust our nuts, but I didn't think it was a good idea. "I think we should just stay here and watch the softball game. Someone could get hurt..." I tried to say, but the stampede to the exit had begun. The others, who gloried in Allen's antics, shouted their approval and in minutes were peddling our bikes at high speed to what they knew would be knee-knocking, heart-stopping fun.

Kiwanis Park Hill was steep and hard to navigate, especially at the high end. It was comprised of five undulating terraces, stretching across the entire length of the park. The hill faced an athletic field that was encircled by a gravel and pitch running track. The Kiwanis Club members who designed the park had created a natural sports amphitheater where people could sit on lawn chairs and blankets to watch community events such as the Lantern Day Parade, amateur football games, or band concerts that took place below. The hill was also a favorite of toboggan and sled aficionados who would soar from terrace to terrace, jumping higher with each leap.

We arrived at the site of our planned descent and lined up along the crest of the hill. Allen proceeded to set the stage for our ride. "We're a posse called the Lone Riders. We've got to get down this hill and save that poor pioneer family down there who are getting their asses whooped by those crazed redskins," he said. "We peddle at full speed and nobody backs out." With that, he tore off down the hill while the rest of us steadied our bikes and our balls.

With Allen waving from below, we each took our turn with a "Hi ho!" and a "Yippee Kiyea!" and a "Jesus Sweet Lord, save me!" The object was to make it to the bottom and coast as far as you could, hopefully reaching the bank of the Sheboygan River in the distance. I watched my four Lone Rider buddies make it to the bottom, a few cheating and cutting a slightly off-center route rather than dropping dead straight down the hill. A few nearly lost control of their bikes, but all managed to make it without causing physical injury to themselves. As they turned from far below I could hear them call to me,

"Come on, Ries, get your ass down here, you little wimp. It's great! It'll do you good, and no fair coasting, you've got to peddle."

I waved, gave the thumbs-up sign, and took off at full speed, successfully making it over the first four terraces. I smelled sweet success as I approached the fifth and final terrace. I saw the athletic field drawing closer. I was home free. My balls and my honor would survive intact. Suddenly my front tire hit an immovable object buried in the grassy hillside—an object I later discovered to be a sprinkler head. My bike, which was going thirty miles an hour, bucked like a horse, throwing me over its outstretched handles toward the surface of the running track below. It happened in seconds. I don't remember somersaulting, but members of my posse attested to the fact that I did a full, laid-out somersault and skidded to a landing on my chest and the right side of my face. As the cloud of cinder dust and gravel settled, I could hear Allen say to the others gathered a short distance away "Shit, what a ride! He da'man! Think he's dead?" The others dropped their bikes and came running to where I lay prostrate.

"Chucky, are you alright? Can you hear me?" my brother Joe asked.

"Chuck, you can get up now. Wow, that was an amazing ride! I never saw anything like that! Your bike is totaled!" my cousin, Mark, said, hoping I could hear him as he knelt beside me rubbing my back gently to make sure I was alive.

I slowly collected my senses and pushed myself up to my knees. I was shaking, and the side of my face burned like a knee that had just kissed concrete. I knew I wasn't dead, but I realized I was hurt. Mark suggested we go to the small field house that also served as a warming shed during winter skating season to see if we could find the janitor whose office was located there.

I didn't want to talk. I wanted some water. Anything to cool the fire that was burning from my forehead down to my chin on the right side of my face. We knocked on the door of the janitor's office and were lucky to find him in. "Hey, mister, my friend fell off his bike and landed on the track. Can you do something for him? Can we call his mom and dad so they can come get him? He's pretty messed up, but he's not dead," Mark observed.

"Well, sure, bring him in, let me have a look," Roy said. We knew his name was Roy because it was stenciled on his shirt pocket. Roy invited us all into his office. It was a collection of cleaning supplies, plumbing tools, and assorted junk that created a cluttered but cozy atmosphere. I knew the prognosis wasn't going to be good when Roy, taking his first look at me, dropped his jaw and opened his eyes as if he'd just seen a ghost. He quickly regained his composure and gave me a pat on the shoulder, saying, "Hey, sonny, it's not so bad. Just a scrape. Shit, I've seen knees skinned worse than your face. You're not even bleeding that much." But I knew he was concealing the truth—a truth he didn't want me to know just yet, at least not until my face stopped burning.

"You come right over here and sit down. I'll fix you up in no time," Roy said. He was a vision in pale green, the uniform of all janitors I have ever known. He chewed the end of a cigar, which had obviously given him pleasure the whole day through. He had a three-day growth of whiskers and a wholesome, friendly demeanor. As Roy invited me to come sit in the chair that was behind his desk, my brother and cousins stood a few feet away, a silent posse of sympathy. "I've got just the medicine you need," he said as he pulled a cold bottle of Coke from an old refrigerator that stood next to his desk and under the Snap-On Tool calendar. Yes, even in mortal pain, my prepubescent eyes couldn't miss the vision that floated above his refrigerator. The Snap-On Tool Miss August.

I took comfort at seeing one of the Snap-On Wonders of the World.

Roy turned and handed me the bottle, saying, "Here you go, junior. This will wet your whistle and get some of that cinder dust out of your throat. It'll help the sting go away. Now I want you to sit real still while I put some medicine on your, ah—face," he said as he cleared his throat, looking again at the massive skin abrasion that occupied his chair. "I must say, sonny boy, I haven't seen anyone manage to get a skin burn on their darn face before. How the hell did you to do that? I mean, what a dumb dog thing to do."

Roy's observation of the obvious wasn't lost on me as I explained my speeding descent down the Kiwanis Hill and my unfortunate collision with one of his sprinkler heads. Roy reached into the First Aid kit he kept in the bottom drawer of his desk, and pulled out a bottle of iodine and a handful of cotton balls. He poured half the bottle onto the cotton balls and dabbed the reddish orange liquid on the right side of my face with the care of an emergency room nurse. I flinched in pain, but I did not cry. I wanted to cry, but I realized that men, even mini-men like me, don't cry. Roy carried out his impromptu medical intervention in about ten minutes, making sure every inch of the wounded area got a healthy dose of iodine. When he finished his job, he said, "You're a tough kid. Your face looks like shit, but nothing seems to be broken. You want to have a look at the goddamn holy mess you've made of yourself?"

My cousins, who had stood silently as Roy tended to my wounds, now came back to life. "Ah, Chuck, maybe you'd better wait till you get home to look at yourself. Let's call your mom and have her come get you," Mark said. I agreed, appreciating the direct counsel of my cousin but wondering why he didn't want me to inspect my face.

In ten minutes my mom arrived to get me in the Chevy truck. She came running into the field house and was taken aback by the vision that stood before her. "Oh, my God! What happened to your face!" she said.

"Ma'am, I think your son flipped his bike while riding down the hill and slid into first base on the side of his face," Roy said, trying to suppress a small laugh. "But I fixed him up."

"I can see that," my mother cried. "Thank you for taking care of him. Oh my God, what happened to you! Just look at your poor face."

I told her I was okay, and seeing my state of bewilderment and pain, she decided not to lecture me about the perils of high-speed descents down Kiwanis Hill.

We were silent during our short ride home. When we arrived, she said, "You'd better take a bath and try to clean your face. You have a bunch of cinder in your skin, so don't rub too hard. It will come out as you heal." I went into the bathroom to wash up and there saw the full glory of my fall. I gasped. My face was a palate of gray, black, red, and iodine orange. I looked like a pothole. I had become the Creature from the Barbecue Pit.

At dinner that night, Jim and John could not resist the temptation to critique my new look and what it reminded them of. "Geez Louise, you look like a hamburger that fell off the grill and into a dirt pile," Jim offered. "Can I charge admission and have my friends come and take a look at you?"

"I've seen worse-looking road kill," John observed after a moment of close inspection.

My mother, ever the pragmatic spirit of love, came flying to my defense. "Just leave him alone," my mother scolded. "Can't you see he looks awful? He knows he looks awful. Think he likes looking that way? He doesn't need you two reminding him what his face looks like!" That night she put cool, wet cloths on my face as I tried to sleep.

My convalescence was short-lived, however, as my mother called to say it was time to get ready for Sunday mass. I asked if, under the circumstances, I could be relieved of my Sunday obligation, but she said, "God doesn't care how ugly we look. He still loves us. You're going to church." I had no choice. There was not a *Sunday mass optional* in my family's list of *What To Do on Sunday Morning*. So I got dressed, and my new face and I went to worship.

Since my family went to the 6:00 a.m. mass and usually got there early enough to get in a little extra praying time, I didn't have to suffer the stares and questions of my parents' friends. I was embarrassed and kept my head down throughout the mass. As I walked to communion, I stuck close behind Jim, using his back to shield me from the looks of those I passed by. I carefully worked my way into position at the communion rail.

From the corner of my eye, I could see the priest working his way down the railing, delivering the host to a series of eager outstretched tongues. Finally he stood before me, his eyes turned toward heaven, holding the sacred consecrated body of my savior aloft. As our eyes met and he saw my face, he uncharacteristically, and a bit too loudly, said, "Body of Christ Almighty, What Happened To Your Face!" rather than the customary "Body of Christ."

My reply was "Amen". A meek, humble, and defeated little *Amen*. After I had taken Jesus on my tongue, I got up from the communion rail and returned to my pew. I lowered my head a bit further than usual that day and prayed, "Oh dear God, heal me quickly and lift this burden from Your faithful and disfigured servant Chuck."

8.

Bill the Mink

"FUCK like a mink?" Just ask me. I can't tell you how many times I've heard this term thrown about by people who have no clue what "fucking like a mink" is all about. But I do. I was there. I have witnessed the pure unadulterated glory of feline fury in the breeding arena. Even before I knew how to do the wild thing or received the mandatory Birds and Bees lecture, I had observed thousands of matched pairs duke it out. It wasn't fucking, but a prelude to high fashion.

We needed our breeding females to give birth in May and early June. Because gestation took eight to nine weeks, we had no choice but to begin breeding in the meanest and sometimes coldest month of the year—March. Each day would bring a new flavor of bad weather: sleet, snow, rain, and the relentless northeast winds that blew off Lake Michigan. Thus, in the worst weather month of the year, the annual rite of Breeding Season was held.

We had over 1,200 matches to facilitate. My father had methodically charted out who the breeding pairs would be, making sure successful matings of the prior year were repeated in order to optimize size, quantity and quality. My father, three brothers, and I, along with the deft-handed and cheerful Marvin, plodded through the rain, sleet, and snow in search of fertility. We were nature's little matchmakers. We'd lug our furtive lovers from cage to cage, doing our best to encourage romance and making sure there were no pretenders.

The process was simple. We'd invite a male mink into a carrying cage and walk him to the designated female. And we'd keep careful watch. Once the deed was done, we'd open the pen top and the triumphant stud would hop back into the carrying cage and be returned home. There he'd relax, have a bite to eat, and then go back to perform his sacred duty.

Most females were cooperative. The seasoned ones had the mating ritual down pat. So for them, we would introduce first-year-breeding rookies and allow them to fumble their way to glory. To the uninitiated first-year females, we introduced our seasoned veterans to make sure all went without mishap or surprise. It was all quite routine. We would freeze our nuts off waiting for them to get their balls off. But inevitably, there would be ten to twenty females who took no interest in their suitors. These furred first-year virgins would try to rip our good-natured breeding males from limb to limb. It was not a pretty sight. The males would beg us to come and get them before their breeding day was over. Many a gallant and determined suitor had to be withdrawn from the field of battle bitten, humiliated, and nearly emasculated. Whoever said breeding was easy never fucked a mink. So as the season wound down we were left with the challenge of breeding these hard-to-get young vixens.

We have all seen the individual or animal who rose far above a particular sport or vocation. The Michael Jordan, Shamu, Itzak Perlman, Bill Gates, and Secretariats of the world. Those phenoms who are not only good at something, but seemingly born to do it. Designed by God for one sacred purpose—a purpose, whose importance is known only by God, but whose glory is viewed with awe by each and every spectator. Riesville had such a mink. One mighty male whose lovemaking prowess was greater than all others—the illustrious and spry Bill the Mink.

Bill's challenge was great, but so too was his ability. Given the task at hand, any thinking mink would have run as far and as fast as his little legs could carry him. But not our hero, not our Bill. This fool rushed in where other mink feared to tread.

We'd drop Bill into these dens of certain destruction and time and again he'd exude the enthusiasm of a mink half his age. Our trained mink-handler ears could almost hear Bill say, "Love will find a way, fellas! Come back in thirty minutes." He always made good on his silent promise. We'd return with hope in our eyes, and sure enough, Bill had delivered. Unlike most breeding males whose shelf life was three to four seasons, Bill brought home the bacon for ten long seasons. I'm not sure what the equivalent of human to mink years is, but I guess it meant Bill was fucking his way around our mink yard well into his nineties. Even as he slowed down and no longer timed his love leaps as he once did, he still hit a few out of the park. And when he could pounce no more, we enshrined him in a corner pen where the sun shone and a westerly breeze gently blew past him as he snoozed and reflected on the glory days of his youth. We'd give him a bit more feed, freshen his water more often than we needed to, and otherwise pamper and venerate this master of love. And unlike his contemporaries, we let him die a natural death.

The good Lord finally took our Bill from us just a few days after we celebrated his thirteenth birthday. Although he had fathered over 856 children, most of them couldn't make his wake, as they were attending operas, black tie balls, and ballets as someone's coat. But my brothers, Marvin, and I were there. We gathered around his cage and sang the old mink a rousing chorus of *For He's a Jolly Good Fellow.* We carried his cold, lifeless body to a shady little spot near the carpenter shop and laid him to rest. We were unusually sentimental for a bunch of minkers that day as we gathered around our hero's tiny grave, each of us sharing his own silent thoughts with our departed friend. As a lasting memorial we placed a small wooden marker over his grave that stated the simple truth about Bill: *He Fucked Like A Mink.*

. . .

My prayerful, God-fearing father gave thanks for each and everyone of his seven children, but I am sure he breathed a loud sigh of relief when his last four children popped out with penises. The final score: five boys, two girls. Numbers sure to bring a smile to a farmer's eyes.

Farm kids begin adult labor at a young age. There is no option. Especially when the farm is family owned and operated. Hiring outside help is expensive and finding experienced help hard to do. The only practical solution to finding cheap skilled labor is to have a large family and, ideally, a good number of sons.

The backbone of my father's work force was his children. Credit for this production line must be placed on the broad and holy shoulders of the Catholic Church and its Mr. Magoo method of family planning. Women who were the faithful practitioners of this method were supposed to know when they were about to ovulate and refrain from intercourse. The male practitioners, on the other hand, just hummed loudly and praised the Lord when the urge to surge came over them. It was a system filled with holes, and as a result, the really good Catholic families won population prizes. In the final years of her life (and after a Brandy Old Fashion), my mother confessed, "What did I know about planning? We just had you whenever you arrived. We did what the church told us to do." She turned to my nieces and said, "You girls have it made. You don't have to have a dozen kids."

If one looked strategically at these results, and put aside the tendency to be cynical, my father and mother had conceived a workforce that would span thirty-five years. Our little army of workers so amused my Uncle Pete, that he called us Carl's Seven Dwarfs. Seven children in fourteen years. Not a bad HR department for a mink farm...*hi ho, hi ho, off to work we go.*

My work career in the mink yard began when I was five years old. At first the tasks assigned to me were simple, repetitive chores like opening and closing mink feeders, filling watering cups with a long garden hose, and scraping day-old feed off the serving trays. After becoming proficient at these tasks, I graduated to hog ringing new pens, mixing and grinding feed, bedding kennels, and of course, the *pièce de résistance*—removing manure from beneath pens. With greater strength and manual dexterity, I joined the gang in grading and pelting.

. . .

Grading was the tedious process of deciding which animals would be kept for breeding and which would be pelted in the fall. Each animal born that year was picked up in early November and personally examined. Excluding those mink that had made the grade the previous season, there were over ten thousand animals to be evaluated. This was a production line operation that needed many hands to complete over a four- to five-day period. Rollie Gimble, his son, and his three grandsons would join us, and we did the same for him. Over the course of two weeks, a roving band of six to ten men would go from ranch to ranch and lug each mink outside to be graded by the man with the best eye for mink in Sheboygan County—my father. He knew what made a mink great. Laying both his hands on the back of the mink, he used his two thumbs to open the guard fur and gaze into it. There he would see a rainbow of colors no one else could—shades of blue or gray. He'd float his hand back and forth over the fur and instantly assess its texture, depth, and evenness. He saw breeding possibilities and future matings. When a real beauty would be brought out, he'd take the time to show me its rich blue-gray color, but I could never see what he saw. I didn't have the *eye*.

Ninety-five percent of my father's herd was rated Black GLAMA (Great Lakes Mink Association), the highest rating a ranch dark mink could be given at the New York Auction Company. The plaques hanging on our dining room wall attested to the quality of Ries mink. When it came to mink fur, my dad's standards were exact and his product top-drawer.

Grading required quick, strong hands. Mink are fast and mean-spirited. Even with double-layered leather gloves, we'd feel the sharp sting of teeth clamping down onto our hands or fingers, usually digging deep enough to draw blood. We carried each animal out of the shed and presented it to my father. We had to move. My father had little patience for anyone, especially his sons, who lost their grip while holding a squirming animal he was inspecting. In order to feel the fur, he didn't wear protective gloves and when a slip happened he'd get an angry animal gnawing on his hand. "Goddamn it, Chucky! Can't you hold that goddamn mink still! For Christ's sake, how many fingers do you think I have? Shit!" he'd shout, waving his finger like it was on fire and squeezing it to stop the blood flow.

Work was the only environment in which my father cursed or lost his temper. In the house he was the Shadow. Outside, he was more of a guy. Marvin and the other older men would roar with laughter. When one of us dropped a mink, they'd join in the fun by directing their own words of wisdom to my brothers and me as, red-faced, we returned to the shed to grab another eight-to-twelve-pound test of our manhood.

"Hey, Chucky, we're just grading them, not trying to French kiss them," Marvin said.

"Marv, you just leave that little guy alone. He's great with the eight-pound girls. It's just the guys who make him nervous. Nothing wrong with being a ladies' man. No sir, he keeps that up and he's going to have a whole harem of black beauties chasing him around the yard trying to kiss his little hinder." Rollie said just loud enough for all to hear.

John had just dropped his sixth mink of the afternoon and was now in hot pursuit. He ran down the long shed, made a diving leap, and grabbed it in his outstretched arms.

"How many does that make, twenty? Hey, Butterfingers, how about we make a bet. Quarter for every one you drop and dollar for every one I drop," Marvin said to him. John was the hardest worker of my father's five sons. He was intense, focused, and humorless, or rather, incapable of being funny even when he tried. He was also a penny-pincher. There wasn't a dollar he'd ever spent that he didn't still miss. He was stocky with sandy brown hair.

"Forget it, I'm not making any more stupid bets with you."

"You could've won twenty bucks last summer, if you hadn't lost your concentration. I guess all the blackberry brandy didn't help clear your head," Marvin said as he reached into another kennel and pulled out a large black male for my dad to grade.

"She slipped. The brandy had nothing to do with it. I had her. She just got away from me. She almost tore me a new asshole," John said.

"She was just giving you a little love peck, but old Uncle Marv saved you from more permanent damage. A couple inches and we'd be calling you *Shorty* instead of *Butterfingers*," Marvin said

. . .

My parents had left for their annual one-week car trip with our church pastor, Father Robert Weller. As always, they left Marvin in charge with Jim and John as his support staff.

Father Weller loved his yearly car trips and his big, fully loaded Oldsmobile. He didn't see a conflict in ministering to the needs of the poor and needy from the soft leather seats of a brand new Oldsmobile. His love of worldly things also included good food and drink. A short, round man in his mid-sixties, he was well taken care of, with a full-time housekeeper and many grateful parishioners who loved to entertain him. He was known for having a short fuse with the mass servers and wasn't shy about letting them know when they'd screwed up. He knew what he liked, and you'd better do it the way he liked it done.

Each summer the church got Father Weller a new set of wheels and, to commemorate the occasion, he would invite my parents to join him on a road trip. The fact that my folks were among the largest contributors to the parish certainly wasn't lost on him.

When Jim and John finally stumbled into the feed house, they were nursing large hangovers from the night before. They'd gone off with Marvin the previous day to bale hay and make some extra money. The routine was always the same—work like a horse for three hours tossing eighty-pound bales of hay and then drink like there was no tomorrow. On this night, Marvin introduced the boys to blackberry brandy—the pancake syrup of alcohol. It didn't take too many shots followed by beer chasers for them to become filled with the joy and warming effects of their latest adventure in booze. Once they were in the bag, Marvin drove them home, rolled them both into bed, and told them he'd be back bright and early in the morning.

True to his word, Marvin pulled up at 7:30 a.m.,

whistling and calling up through the open screen door on the second floor porch, "Hey you two knuckleheads, get your butts out of bed, it's time to work. You're not on vacation this week. You're working for me." A short time later, Tweedledee and Tweedledum emerged from the house wearing the same clothes they'd worn the night before. Slow-moving, large-headed, speechless, and each wearing sunglasses.

"Johnny, water the mink. Jimmy, you start grinding feed," Marvin ordered, and the day began. It was mid-June, and the females had just had their litters. This put them in the worst mood of the year—frantic, agitated, and as protective as any mother would be of her young.

Marvin was checking bedding and called to my brother, who was filling watering cups, "Johnny, come over here. I'll show you what fast looks like." Both brothers walked over and saw a female that was sleeping outside her kennel. "Now, watch closely and observe." Marvin rolled up his shirtsleeve like a magician to show he wasn't hiding anything, slowly and quietly opened the pen door, reached down, and quickly grabbed the female by the back of the neck. No doubt about it—Marvin was fast and strong. The mink saw red. Twisting and turning, she tried to break free and rip into whatever it was that was holding the back of her neck. Lifting the flaying female at an arm's length away from him, he instructed his beginner's class, "Don't ever try to do this without adult supervision. It takes nerves of steel to pick up a sleeping female who just had her kittens. It's like jumping into a pool of sharks with a roast beef sandwich." He waited a moment longer to make sure his students had fully absorbed the morning's lesson and then dropped the enraged female back into her pen.

Despite their duller-than-usual minds, both my brothers were entertained and fascinated. Typically, we set feed boards in front of each kennel to make it easier for the young kittens to crawl out and eat. To clean the board, we'd reach in through the pen, scrape off the old feed into a bucket we carried around our waist, and then move quickly to the next pen. On our scraping hands, we wore double-layered leather gloves and fastened four or five pieces of thin sheet metal over the fist. It was like wearing a suit of armor on one's hand. The female would attack the glove, bounce off, and we'd quickly move down the aisle.

"How much you want to bet I could do that?" John, the brother with the least swollen head, asked.

"How about the money you'll make baling hay tomorrow?" Marvin offered.

"Too, much." John, ever the thrifty and risk-averse

gambler replied. "How about half the money I make baling hay tomorrow?"

"Sure, Johnny. It's a deal," Marvin said.

The three of them walked down the aisle looking for another sleeping female. As John opened the pen door, Marvin and Jim looked on. Unlike Jim, John was not a total dummy. He was focused and careful. He had good hands, which usually benefited from being in leather catching gloves.

With a quick lunge, he grabbed the female behind her neck. She fought like a large Walleye on the end of a fishing line. Slapping, twisting, balling up, and scratching his arms with her claws. The scratches didn't matter, we were used to them. What mattered was winning the bet. "Got you, you little shit!" He said triumphantly, turning to Marvin and Jim to show his prize a moment too soon.

"Ahhhh, ahhhh, oh shit….ahhhhh!!!! My finger! She's got my finger!" John screamed. The look on his face quickly turned from triumphant gloating to abject pain.

"Well, ask her to let go. Say, 'Please, Ms. Minky, will you let go of my finger?'" Marvin suggested as he and Jim cried with laughter at the sight of John running down the aisle with a pissed-off mink attached to the end of his finger.

"Help! Shit! Oh, please help me. Damn!" John shouted

as he continued to run swinging the female in circles at his side. He looked like he was doing a rope trick, but the rope was alive and firmly clamped down on his index finger. John made a loop around the aisle and returned to Marvin, "Please, do something! You win, damn you! There, you happy? I'll pay the bet, just get this thing off my finger!"

Marvin took the metal scraper in his hand and tapped the female lightly on her head. He didn't want to hurt her, just break her concentration. She fell to the ground. John looked relieved. His finger was bleeding badly and his honor was in tatters, but he was done with her. The only problem was she wasn't done with him, and she proceeded to snap at his ankles, setting his feet to dancing. John's mink yard jig became a good deal more animated when she nimbly ran up his pant leg. John once again took off running, arms raised, hands waving, and screaming a litany of swear words. Like a heat-seeking missile, she'd worked her way up his pant leg. A swarm of horrific possibilities ran through young John's mind. "Help me! Please! Oh, shit. Oh, God! Oh, God no! She's going to get my nuts. Help me!"

Sensing the urgency of the moment, Marvin ran alongside John, who had dropped his pants faster than any man ever dropped his drawers at a full run. It was a sight to see, Olympic in its athleticism. As he ran, the female who had now found pay dirt was resolutely attached to his ass. Running behind John, Marvin again conked the female on the head, grabbed her barehanded as she fell to the ground, and took her back to her pen.

John's ass and finger healed, but he lost twenty dollars and would forever be called Butterfingers.

9.

The Wisdom
of the River

ALL WORK took place in the *mink yard*. The mink
yard was situated just one hundred feet east of our back
door. Commuting was never easier.

A simple four-foot high guard fence encircled the yard.
It was made of chicken wire that was strung between
heavy fence posts and had an aluminum cap on the top
to keep animals from jumping over. It surrounded the
entire yard. In the yard were the livestock pens. Since
mink are stealthy animals, repairing the guard fence and
mending pens was a priority. Each of our fur-bearing
friends was money on the paw, and preventing escapes
was a constant concern.

Some of you may have qualms about raising animals for their fur. Animal lovers view it as barbaric. Raising animals for food is one thing, but raising them to wear is quite another. I admit I too had philosophical misgivings about my family's line of work, but I gained some solace when I considered how hard my father labored to make the short lives of his mink as happy as he could. In his own way, he loved his mink. In fact, he seemed to fuss over them a great deal more then he did his own children. He certainly spent more time with them than he did with us. So when it came time for them to give him the shirt off their back, they did so with minimal protest, as the fall from consciousness was swift, painless, and—I hope—stress free.

Our mink yard covered an area of three acres. It was divided into two broad areas. One held all the pens we used to breed and raise young mink. The other held the sheds used to house mink as they grew to adulthood and needed separate quarters. We had twenty-four sheds that were one hundred fifty feet long with corrugated aluminum roofs. Each shed housed three hundred mink. In the open yard area we had two thousand pens. These were aligned in forty rows, two hundred feet long, each row holding fifty pens. A pen was enclosed with chicken wire on three sides as well as the bottom. This allowed air to circulate, and feces to fall through the pen bottom. At the rear of each pen was a kennel with a food tray and watering cup at the front. The goal was to create a living environment that would not spoil or stain the fur. The tops of the pens were covered in corrugated aluminum, and each had a large, latched trapdoor that allowed us to reach in and feed, move, and otherwise care for the animals.

We walked the gravel-covered aisles that ran between the rows of pens many times each day. These footpaths would become slick, muddy, and smelly when we had long periods of rain or the snow began to melt. The mess was made worse by the overflow from the watering cups, which needed to be filled two to three times a day. Despite these obstacles, we forged on, wading through muck so gelatinous it sometimes sucked our rubber boots right off. We were minkers; mud wasn't going to stop us.

Fur-bearing animals, even in the wild, live on a high-fat, high-protein diet. The diet of a domestically raised mink consists of a wide range of meat, poultry, cheese, and fish products. Every week we would unload semi-trailers filled with fifty-pound blocks of whale meat, condemned rabbits, chickens, cow, and horsemeat as well as cheese products. We'd get three hundred-pound barrels filled with fish oil and corn oil, and thousands of fifty-pound bags of dry cereal from National Foods. We'd get regular deliveries of cow stomachs, livers, and any edible part of a cow, sheep, or goat that a butcher couldn't sell to humans. All of this would be run through an industrial-size grinder and then into a vast mixer that could wipe up three tons of high-protein feed that had the consistency of oatmeal.

. . .

Three times a month my father and I would drive to the commercial fishing shanties that lined the Sheboygan River. Fishing boats would dock here and unload Lake Perch, salmon, and other edible fish. We'd come for the chubs. Chubs are garbage fish that grew in abundance in Lake Michigan and, while not suited for human consumption, were perfectly good in mink food. We'd take them home, put them into fifty-pound pans, and freeze them for use throughout the month. My father's walk-in freezer was thirty feet by twenty feet square with a twenty-foot ceiling. It could hold several hundred tons of frozen food products.

"Dad, I'm not feeling good," I said one day. I had a

low-grade fever, a runny nose, and body aches. "How about getting Joe to go with you?"

"Joe's bedding mink. Doesn't look like you're dying. You're coming," he said.

I gathered my life forces, jumped up into the pickup truck, and headed off with my dad to the docks for a chub run. It was a cold rainy day in early spring. We backed the truck up onto the loading scale, and my father went to the office window a short distance away to settle up for the fish. As he did the paperwork, I worked with Leon Heinmeister shoveling chubs into large wooden crates that lined the floor of the pickup. I'd worked with Leon before. He was a red-faced man in his mid-fifties with a medium build and a prizewinning beer belly. Leon let his beard grow wild throughout the year and shaved it off on New Year's Day, right after the Polar Bear Club plunged into Lake Michigan. "It's good luck to start the year off with a good intention and a clean face. Hell, maybe this'll be the year I find that little lady to take care of ole' Leon."

Leon was wearing the same outfit he always wore— yellow rubber work pants held up by suspenders, black knee-high rubber boots, a tattered, red flannel shirt, and a blaze orange stocking cap that he wore year-round no matter the weather. He called it his "Lucky Bucky" cap, and he would tell anyone who'd listen of his many victories during Wisconsin's state holiday, *Deer Hunting Season.* "I tell you, kid, that buck was at least a thirty-pointer—huge, more like a Brahma bull than a deer, really. Anyway, it was the biggest deer this sure-eyed man of the woods has ever seen. So, there I am. Out of bullets. It's just man against beast, and he starts to charge me—and I don't mean for the three hamburgers I'd had for lunch either. He lowers his head and comes tearing after me. Well shit, I'm not nuts; I turned tail and ran my ass into the woods. No way he's going to fit that rack of his into those woods. But sure as shit if that big dumb beast doesn't come thundering after me, thrashing his way through pine trees, raising hell and bearing down on yours truly. Well, you know what I did? I remembered I had some deer scent in my pocket. You know what deer scent is, don't you kid?"

"No, Mr. Heinmeister," I replied as I kept shoveling. With Leon, I always did all the shoveling.

"Well, it's love juice—if you know what I mean. You're old enough to know that deer hunting season is right smack dab in the middle of mating season, aren't you?"

"Mr. Heinmeister, my dad raises mink. I know a thing or two about breeding seasons."

"Oh, sure. 'Course you do. So I pour some of the love juice in my hat—the very hat you see me wearing today. Hey, I'm no spring chicken. I'm getting pretty damn pooped out at about this point. But what have I got to lose? I figure, 'Shit, if this don't do it, Leon, you are a piece of Swiss cheese.' So I pour the whole bottle of love sauce in my cap and toss it over my shoulder. Just like this," he said, demonstrating with great effect his heroic wilderness throw. "And you know what? Why, Jesus in heaven if that cap doesn't land right on top of that buck's fire-breathing nostrils. I swear. As God is my witness, it landed right on his deer damn nose! It was like I hit him with a ton of bricks. He stops in his tracks and kind of gets all misty-eyed. Must have thought he'd just been kissed by two of the biggest, sweetest set of doe lips in Krushski's Woods. Shit, I don't know. But he stands there and keeps staring at me all dreamy-like. I think, maybe he thinks I'm looking pretty cute right about then and I'd better watch my sweet little ass or that's going to look like Swiss cheese too. But son-of-gun if that stud doesn't just raise up on his hind legs like Hi Ho Silver, kicking his front hooves up in the air and giving me the biggest, loudest bray I'd ever heard. I guess he was thanking me and waving good-bye or something. Shit, I don't know. But he turns and heads back in the direction he came, leaving nothing behind but this cap you see on my head." Leon stopped, removed his cap, stared at it as if it were a sacred relic, and caressed it fondly with his nose while inhaling its wilderness scent. It wasn't a hat. It was his crown of gold. "That's why I call it my 'Lucky Bucky' cap...Chucky." He finally said, using my name to good effect since it rhymed with his favorite topic of dockside conversation.

Resting for a moment, Leon realized I wasn't shoveling at full speed and said, "Hey, come on there, junior. Get your ass in gear or this'll take all day." He said, without a hint of irony. "You feeling okay, kid? You look a little green around the gills."

"I've got the flu or something. I'm okay. Hey, Dad, you got a hanky? I have to blow my nose." I shouted over to the office window.

My dad turned to answer, but before he could reply, Leon did. "Fishermen don't use hankies, son. God gave' em a permanent hanky. Just like He gave us noses, He gave us all a hanky. Bet you didn't know that?"

"No, Mr. Heinmeister, I didn't. Where is it? I could sure use one right about now," I said, my nose now running like a river.

"Why, the damn thing is right here in your left hand,"

Leon said. Standing knee-deep in chubs, he put his shovel aside and raised his right hand to the sky, assuming the pose young Prince Hamlet took as he gazed blankly into the eyes of the lofted skull, pondering his woeful existence. With his left hand, Leon began to thoughtfully massage the end of his chin as if he were trying to remember something. Trying to divine some lost seafaring truth. After a moment he surprised me when he proclaimed, "To blow or not to blow, that is the question. Why, what the hell—I think I'll let her blow!" Lowering his left hand, he pinched his nostrils slightly, bent over, and let rip with one of the biggest gale force hoots I'd ever seen. It was impressive—simple and practical, the perfect frontier solution to no hanky. I'd never seen anyone do it before. He stood up, placed his hands on his hips, and proudly said, "That's what me and me friends call the Fisherman's Cheer. Now, matey, let Captain Leon give you another little tip. Always blow with your left hand and never into the wind. You got that? Only use your left hand."

"Why is that, Mr. Heinmeister?"

"Well, you little rummy, it's because you eat with your right hand. Shit, you don't want to be blowing your goddamn nose with the hand you eat with, do you?"

It was all coming too fast. I was trying to remember the instructions he was giving me. I didn't want to lose a detail. This was good stuff. I would take it home and share it with the gang. I'd never considered the nuances of a Fisherman's Cheer before.

Proud of having passed on one of the secret legacies of lake fishermen to a twelve-year-old landlubber, Leon looked at me one last time. He cocked his head to the right, squinted his left eye like Long John Silver, and said, "Well, matey, you ready to use the hanky God gave us sea-faring pirates and blow that little schnozzola of yours?"

"Yes sir, I'm ready." I gave it all I had. I did it twice. It worked great. He was right; God did give me hanky to go with my large Ries nose.

On the way home my dad asked how I was doing and I told him, "Under the circumstances, this was one of the best chub runs I ever took with you. Mr. Heinmeister is a pretty cool guy. I thought he was just another stupid dock worker, but he turned out to be a really cool guy."

"Never judge people by what they look like, Chucky. There are plenty of people better off than we are who choose to dress like bums, drive beat-up trucks, and live in ordinary homes. What matters is what people have in their head and in the bank. It's called German poor. We like our money in our pockets and not on our backs," he said as we pulled up in front of the feed house.

I wasn't quite sure what to make of my dad's lecture on German character. But I was pretty sure Leon Heinmeister had neither brains in his head nor money in his pocket, but none of that mattered. I had valuable life information to share, and I ran out into the mink yard eager to show my brothers and Marvin a brand new cheer.

. . .

Death during pelting season was quick and painless. We'd drop our mink into a medium-sized wooden box with a small trapdoor on the top. Inside was a wire floor that slanted down toward a hinged side door. Under the wire floor we placed two aluminum pizza trays onto which we sprinkled cyanide powder. The irritated animal would be dropped into the box where it found quick eternal rest, its little soul rising to heaven so that its pelt could be used to keep ladies wearing pearls warm. We'd drop twenty mink into the "sleeping box," one at a time. We would wait a few minutes, and then, holding our breath, open the side door and let the lifeless animals tumble into a wheelbarrow that had been layered in hay for a soft post-life landing. We would then wheel them into the carpenter shop—a rustic, cream brick building that was a historic remnant of my grandfather's dairy farm. It was there that my father and Marvin would skin the animals, pulling their hides off in much the same manner one might remove a skin-tight sweater. We'd then stretch the hides on boards and place them in the freezer to cool down. Since the fat that clung to the hide froze faster than the hide itself, freezing made it easier to scrape the fat off in a process called *fleshing*. When this was complete, we carried the freshly scraped hides into the basement of our home, tacked them to drying boards, and let them sit overnight. In the morning we'd wipe the mink oil off with a cotton towel, after which each hide would be stamped with my father's ranch seal and boxed for shipment to the New York Auction Company. There they'd be bundled into groups of one hundred, based on similar characteristics—size, gender, color, sheen—and sold to the highest bidder. All hail fashion!

Thanksgiving fell right in the midst of pelting season. We were frantic to get the harvest in at exactly the moment our mink were coming into their first full winter coat. Despite our busy schedule my mother insisted that we attend the annual Thanksgiving Day celebration at her sister's home in Sheboygan. By the time we arrived at 3:00 p.m., Uncle Pete, his six kids, my Aunt Mary, and her husband were waiting for us. The Rieses always arrived late and left early.

We'd cleaned up, washed our hands, and changed our clothes. But we couldn't change our smell. Our good-hearted city cousins, who pitied our lifestyle, would never make a nasty comment. But they were well aware of the cloud that traveled with us. Our trained minker eyes could detect their controlled grimaces as the *eau de mink* wafted their way—particularly during pelting season. Mink have odor glands. Like skunks, these glands are activated when they are angry or frightened.

"How's my favorite cuz doing!" my cousin Joan said to Jim as she winced slightly. After another moment to regain her composure, she continued. "Smells like... I mean, looks like you're in full swing. You poor guys, seems like you have to work all the time," she said as we took our positions at the card table set up for the younger kids to enjoy holiday dinner. "You know we pity you. I mean, we love you, but we also pity you. Aren't you sick of working all the time?"

"It's a life sentence," Jim replied, stuffing his mouth full of food. "We were born to the wrong father. I'd trade ten of my dad for one of yours. But hey, you have to take the cards God deals you and look at the positive side of things; we get to swoop in here, stink the place up, and then split right after dessert so we can knock off a few hundred more mink before midnight. How many kids can you point to and say, 'He just killed five hundred mink today'? Joan, you lucked out when you got Uncle Pete as your dad. Well, I'll just have to put in my time with the patron saint of slave drivers," Jim rambled on.

. . .

The diet we fed our animals produced the best ranch dark mink in America. It also created some of the best shit in America. Ries mink manure could turn a simple backyard garden into a lush tropical paradise. Our manure was so sought-after that it became known as "Minker's Miracle Grow: Just one bushel basket and your underachieving garden problems are over!" Family, friends, and strangers came for a bushel basket or two to go. But its potency demanded they use it sparingly, not only because of what it did to their gardens, but because of how it made their gardens smell.

And while our neighbors hated the smell, the flies gloried in it. Entire swarms moved to our farm. If I had been a fly, I'd have done the same. Such a deal! Plenty of day-old, high-protein shit to revel in. Welcome to Riesville! Please hold your nose. Watch where you step, and swat that fly.

I didn't smell a thing. I had been genetically engineered to thrive in this environment that often overloaded the senses. But it only took the visit of a close friend or relative to remind me that we weren't raising orchids. "God almighty, it stinks around here! How do you stand it?" they would ask.

It was an earthy way to grow up. Each season brought a new set of chores, more slogging through the mud, more flies, more frostbite. Our perfectly ordered existence ran like clockwork and resulted in the best mink money could buy.

10.

Catholic Boy

I PRAYED hard. I believed in a God that heard my prayers. If I asked long and hard enough, God would grant me any desire. This faith burned in me like a passionate love affair. I knew that when I spoke to my Lord with steely determination and unwavering faith, He heard me.

As time passed and my thinking became more complex, it dawned on me that He often—in fact, most of the time—didn't hear me. The ten-speed bike never appeared at the side of my bed when I woke in the morning. I continued to get C's while I prayed for A's, and I didn't appear to be getting any better looking. But these and other prayerful disappointments didn't shake my belief that relief was just a prayer away. When the nuns tried to temper my enthusiasm by explaining, "God only grants those requests that are good for us," I didn't buy it. Yes, in class I nodded my head in agreement, but in my heart I knew God would give me anything I asked for. I just had to ask harder. I just wasn't asking well enough. If I focused the full might of my mind and heart, clenched my fists, and squeezed my eyes in concentrated devotion, I could, and would, receive the miracles I asked for.

To this day I carry this faith in me. While it has been tempered with the disappointments of adulthood and life in general, I still see the face of God in my blunders and my many blessings. I believe that no matter how crazy life becomes, there is always some goodness in it, and that when I look back over my life from heaven, I will know exactly what that goodness was.

Such zealousness had to be nurtured, watered, and pruned in order to grow such deep roots and withstand the inherent absurdities of blind faith and popular culture. And it was into such a God-loving oven that I was born and baked into a good Catholic boy.

. . .

My parents were tireless when it came to God and

Church. They read the Good Book and stuck to its rules like rats on a life raft. Even when the rules were patently absurd, they wouldn't waver. They believed in the sanity of the church and the wisdom of its elders. They were the best foot soldiers God's army ever had.

"Kids, it's time for church!" came my mom's voice from downstairs. It was still dark outside when preparations began. Like bath time, mealtime, and just about any time, it was an epic undertaking. Everyone had to be wearing his or her Sunday best—boys in suits and ties, and girls in dresses. It didn't matter that it was sub-zero and a blizzard outside, the Rieses would be at Sunday 6:00 a.m. mass on time and looking like they just stepped out of the Sears and Roebuck Catalogue.

We boys each applied a hair treatment called "goop." Goop had the consistency of syrup and concretized hair in seconds. Once applied, hair became impervious to all wind and storm conditions. Its application was simple. I'd dip my comb into the green syrup, accumulate a good globule's worth, and quickly apply it with a flip, twist, and a flop of the wrist—the result being a pleasant frontal hair wave. Besides holding hair in place, goop had the side benefit of giving me something to do during mass. I'd run my fingers through my hair, returning goopified hair clusters to their normal soft texture. Simple pleasures, but distractions that meant everything during an hour-long mass.

The Rieses were never late for mass. Though packed to the gunwales in our 1956 Chevy, we'd be in our prayer positions just as the priest waltzed into the sanctuary for the start of the show. We made up half of the early mass population. I don't think it would have started without us. It would have been a bit like a plane taking off without its passengers.

Just as bath night taught us to suffer in silence no matter how cold and cloudy the water was, being roused out of bed at 5:00 a.m. for 6:00 a.m. mass taught us that the only worthwhile profession was working full time for God. And we knew it was true, because God told us so— in our heads. *I will turn every child of Carl and Helen Ries into a nun or a priest. No Ries child shall be spared. I want them all. They're all mine. Mine, mine, mine!* And who argues with God? Three had already signed up, and God saw four more strong recruits cooking in Carl and Helen's soul kitchen. Scoring seven out of seven would put us in a mythological stratosphere all our own.

My parents' early successes made more secular members of our congregation flee at the sight of us. They feared we carried a vocational virus. While this was just nasty, cruel thinking, there was no doubt that my parents had hard-wired each of their young, half-awake children with the ability to tune into the signal emanating from the tabernacle on the altar. This gold-plated box that housed the body of Christ transmitted a celestial radio signal directly into the minds of His specially chosen few. The great prophets and messengers all heard God's voice and, after receiving Holy Communion, so did I. *Yes, young seed of Ries, you will be my soldier of righteousness, you will heal the sick and feed the poor and have nuns take care of your every worldly need. You too will drive a large Oldsmobile, drink sacred wine, and have wonderful meals served unto you.* I'm sure my siblings were having the same conversation with God in the quiet of their heads.

By 5:45 a.m., we were in our suits, ties, baby blankets, boots, coats, mittens, and lined up for the march out to the car where my dad was waiting. He was always waiting. No matter what the destination, it was guaranteed that he'd be in the car honking the horn, reminding the eight stragglers to please hurry it up. He felt that it was his duty to get us places on time, but it was not his duty to help us dress. The division of domestic responsibilities was clearly defined, and dressing the kids for mass or other special outings was not on my dad's list.

Once a Catholic, always a Catholic. I have known good Buddhists who were Catholics in a previous lifetime and were still coping with the guilt. The *I-am-not-worthy* attitude and the raging sexuality are by-products of the Catholic-making machine. Truth is, there is no exorcism mighty enough to dispel the Church once it gets its hooks into a young, open mind. That early synaptic wiring never disconnects. It's a bit like Alcoholics Anonymous: You are always one sin away from one more sin. The effects of this blessed brainwashing stain a soul forever. There is no way out of the club.

But it takes more than just daily mass and religion class to mint a gold-plated Catholic. It takes a 360-degree, 24/7 effort. At home there must be daily rosary and the *Bishop Fulton J. Sheen Show* on Sundays. The house must overflow with nuns and priests who are invited for free eats and drinks. Add to this the numerous church boards, volunteer committees, and organizations devoted to promoting religious vocations, and there was no room for the devil in our home. My parents had built an invincible wall that was strong, high, and Catholic.

. . .

My adolescence brought with it the usual sexual desires and yearnings. All good, healthy feelings for a young man to be experiencing except for the fact that such desires were illegal immigrants in my Catholic body, burglars hell-bent on breaking God's law and driving me crazy. To have desire was a sin. To pleasure oneself was a sin. To talk about sex or look at dirty pictures (even naked women in *National Geographic*) was a sin. In fact, desire of almost any kind was viewed as a sin. There is just no room in God's temple (that's me) for sin. But, alas, a life without a little bit of sin is like French fries without catsup.

The outlook for my having a joy-filled life was looking pretty bleak. A sinless life doesn't leave much room for fun or dealing with the biological flooding that passes through a boy at adolescence. The surging hormones, the impromptu hard-ons, and the closet of repressed desires that every nun and priest tries to keep closed. A Catholic boy's imagination is fertile ground for lustful thoughts. It's a classic flesh-versus-the-will-of-God conflict. Hard enough to know which side of that battle one is on as an adult, but pour all this turmoil into the pulsating, awakening body of a twelve-year-old boy and it can be downright earthshaking.

. . .

"Forgive me Father, for I have sinned. It has been ten minutes since my last confession."

Confession was always a good way to kill a few minutes during the grind of daily mass. All classes, first through eighth, would file over to church, which was just a short walk from the grade school. The youngest students would sit in front and the oldest in back. These daily exposures were intended to fan the fire of our faith. But no priest who ever raised a wafer or turned water into wine could raise this rite of boredom to anything but an hour to get through.

I would begin preparing for mass long before departure. I'd smear a thin layer of Elmer's Glue to the back of my hands so that, once I got to church, I could peel it off, round the glue into miniature projectiles, line them up on the top of the pew, and fire when ready. The more self-flagellating members of my class would spend the hour sticking a safety pin through the soft skin that stretched between their thumb and forefinger. Anyone caught in an act of non-prayerful activity was grabbed by the ear, dragged to the back of the class, and forced to sit next to the head nun. But no distraction stood taller or was more sought-after than confession.

Going to confession was the golden calf of the *dead hour*. It allowed the restless young Catholic to get out of the pew and stand in a line that often stretched twenty to thirty students long. I would line up against the marble sidewall of the church and view the less fortunate sheep, who were trapped in their pews twitching and fidgeting with boredom.

Since fifth graders were relatively new to sinning, most penances were of the basic variety—a couple Hail Marys and a few Glory Be To The Fathers were all you needed to make your soul luminous and Godly-white again. The range of things that fell into the sin category was wide and generous. This made coming up with a good long list of sins every few days pretty easy to do, even for an underachieving sinner. Some of my favorites included "I had impure thoughts five times," "I got angry at my brother when he spit at me twice," "I burped in class once," "I spit at my brother three times," "I had angry thoughts about my teacher once," "I had idle and unprayful thoughts during mass six times," "I stole a few quarters from my dad's coin jar five times," and "I swore at my brother three times." The admission of these minor offenses would be followed, depending on the priest—and whether or not he was sleeping—by a few questions about the grievousness of the sins you had confessed and some fatherly advice about not spitting or swearing at your brother. It was a pretty simple sin-for-penance deal that lasted about ten minutes and was repeated every week. The goal was to allow budding young Catholics to confess sins as often as they liked. So often, in fact, that they began to make sins up with the net result being everything was a sin, and guilt was as much a part of life as eating or sleeping. Soon our minds were manufacturing sins and mixing real and imagined infractions into a theological muddle.

I had no problem with any of it. It all worked pretty well for me until the SEX thing raised its ugly head. I couldn't avoid it. God knows I tried not to notice it. But there it was—SEX. It entered my dreams and my waking fantasies. It walked with me along the edge of the YMCA pool on family swim night as I gazed down the swimsuit tops of moms hanging on the side rails. It even followed me on a frozen gravel road that I walked with my cousin, Terry, early one evening in January on our way to the skating rink. Terry was a year older than me and lived next door. An adventurous soul, he introduced me to *Mad* magazine and farting on cue. While I kept my sex demon safely locked within me, he had no qualms about sharing long monologues about this, his favorite topic, "Man, I can't wait to wrap my hands 'round a pair of pulsating boobs. Did you see how big Mary Michael's knockers are getting? Jesus, what a gift," he'd ramble as we read *Mad* up in his bedroom while holding an unlit cigarette between his lips.

Roosevelt Park was about a mile walk from my house and each winter they flooded the field to create a skating rink. As Terry and I walked down the gravel road that ran alongside our farm, he noticed a magazine in the ditch. Curious to see what it was, he jumped down the slight embankment to get it. He hit pay dirt. It was an issue of *Playboy*. Being a bit more advanced than I was, Terry didn't hesitate to start thumbing through its pages. As one moonlit picture after another came into view, he moaned, "Oh, will you look at that one. Wow! Geez, what a set of jugs she's got. This is awesome. What luck. Wonder why someone would want to throw this out the window," Terry said.

I, on the other hand, was torn between the urge to stare *(my lower self)* and make Terry toss this gift from the devil back into the gutter from whence it came *(my higher self)*. Thanks to my cousin's more worldly view and his denying my grasping attempts to seize the magazine and toss it back into the ditch, we spent a good fifteen minutes studying this most remarkable textbook on human anatomy. What choice did I have? He wasn't going to let me throw it away and he wasn't going anywhere, so I was forced to review the entire contents of this remarkable picture book. Little did I know that out of little acorns do mighty oak trees grow, for I could not free my mind from those pictures. They slept with me at night. They provoked me into spontaneous erections and profoundly complicated my young Catholic psyche.

But the temptations didn't stop there. The devil had finally wormed his way into my soul. He had found my hot button and continued to tempt me with more SEX. How cunning is the devil? He seeks out our weakness and then plasters it all over the place. While watching TV, I came upon a special on topless bars. During this hard-hitting news exposé, they blacked out the eyes and breasts of the waitress being interviewed. But I knew very well what was behind the tape. I could see with my developing x-ray vision the fertile pay dirt that lay beneath. My manhood could not be contained. It rose up from its slumber and shot forth. My erotic zone had a feather trigger. The devil had me by the balls and he wasn't letting go. Jesus, Mary, and Joseph couldn't save me now.

The next week I didn't jump into the confession line. I was heavy with sin. I'd had a breakout week. I knew I had to fess up and come clean with my Lord. After a lot of self-dialogue, I finally plucked up the courage, assumed my place in the sinner's line, and waited my turn to enter the confessional. Before there was anything I could do, The Holy Spirit had guided me to the confessional of our Pastor, Father Robert Weller. If I'd been more careful, I'd have lined up on the other side of the church where one of the younger and more laissez-faire priests listened to sins. The new generation of priests was beginning to think that sin was becoming an outmoded idea. But my sin-filled panic had placed me in the wrong line. I had no choice but to enter the darkened confessional and seek forgiveness.

"Forgive me, Father, for I have sinned. It has been two weeks since my last confession," I sprinted through the obligatory opening statement.

"What sins do you have for me today?" I could see the shadowy outline of Father Weller through the small screen that separated us. I clung to the sidewall of the confessional like a criminal. I hoped he couldn't see me through the opaque curtain that separated us. I lowered my voice just a bit to make sure he didn't recognize me, but I felt sure he had me. The priests all knew the Ries boys. Shit, they practically lived at our house, drank our beer, ate our food, and we all served mass for them. I was sure Weller knew exactly who this penitent was.

"I got angry at my brother. I had impure thoughts. I swore at my cousin. I took four quarters from my dad's coin jar. I looked at impure pictures. I talked back to my mom and didn't help an old lady cross the street when I could have." I raced through a list of real and made up sins hoping I'd buried the sexual misconduct sin well enough so Weller's tired old ears wouldn't pick it up.

"So, tell me a bit more about the impure pictures you saw."

"Huh?"

"The impure pictures. Tell me about the impure pictures."

"Ah, well, what do you want to know about them?"

"Where did you see them? What were they? What happened to you when you looked at them?" came the muffled reply from the other side of the screen.

I was sweating. I was trapped like a rat between my growing sex cravings and sin. Caught between the need to tell the whole truth and wanting to tell a big fat lie to escape the inquisition. *Lie? In confession! Oh, God help me. But why should I tell this old fart about my greatest moment? Why should I let him plunder the perfection of angels coming down and kissing me with the sweetest secret of all?* I knew that if I told a lie in confession I'd be damned forever, but I didn't care. I liked sex! Still I couldn't make myself tell Weller what my eyes had gulped down like a gallon of Kool-Aid on a 90-degree day. Sure, I'd sinned, I knew that, but I liked it. I wanted to do it again, and again, and again, but twelve years of moral development had convinced me it was wrong and sinful too, but God in heaven, it was glorious.

I decided to take the minimal approach to confessing my sin, "I saw a *Playboy* magazine and a show about topless waitresses."

"Oh. Well, what did the pictures look like? Can you describe them to me?" At this point a dawning realization (or perhaps it was the Holy Spirit) broke over me and I realized he was along for the ride. He *wanted* the details. I swallowed hard and let it fly. As I chattered on I could feel the beast growing between my legs. I gave Father Weller all the juice I had. I filled his glass to overflowing and during my five-minute monologue, he didn't butt in. With an overheated sigh, I concluded my story and waited for the verdict.

"Five Our Fathers and ten Glory Bes to Jesus, your sins are forgiven."

"Huh. What. That's all?" I blurted out in relief, feeling like a total fool for saying it.

"Yes, go forth and sin no more, and try not to look at any more dirty pictures."

I had broken through. I still felt the weight of sin on my soul. I renewed my commitment to never ever sin again, but the door had been opened. Weller's softball penances were all the incentive I needed. I began to give Mr. Big the hand-job treatment more often and hair didn't grow in my offending palm nor did my teeth fall out as Sister Jean Marie had said they would. And again, I realized that just because a nun or a priest says something is so, doesn't make it so. The first small seeds of my sexual liberation had been sown by the most unlikely of allies.

. . .

But true liberation did not come easily in my journey. I still became debilitated when my pile of sins had grown too high. My condition grew particularly acute when Father Brager, one of the other parish priests, zeroed in on the topic during a sermon one day. He explained to the assembled school children that taking communion while in the state of mortal sin would guarantee a person a one-way pass to hell. My dilemma was made all the more critical because I was not completely certain whether repeated masturbation was a mortal sin *(die and go to hell)* or a venial sin *(die and go to purgatory for a few weeks)*. I needed to ask an expert, but feared seeking the counsel of a priest or a nun. I was walking a theological tightrope and if I didn't watch my step I might end up in hell—forever. Father Brager's sermon had fanned my paranoid confusion.

The week prior to hearing this sermon I'd spanked the monkey more than usual. It was new. It felt great. I did it all the time. Father Brager made it vaguely clear that certain sins of the flesh were mortal and that in the state of mortal sin one could not receive Holy Communion. "Moreover, if you receive the Lord in Holy Communion while in the state of sin, the host will burn a hole in your tongue. Everyone is going to know you're a mortal sinner. So children, why even try to fake God and go to communion like you're a normal person, because when the smoke starts billowing out of your mouth, everyone is going to know you're GUILTY." Well, he got my attention with that little story. I felt pretty certain this was another bogus admonition designed to scare the shit out of me just to keep me from sinning, but how could I be sure?

As I sat in the pew with my thirty-five classmates, the time to receive communion was quickly approaching. I could feel my bladder tighten. I was panicked. I had to pee. I felt that if I didn't go I would burst, so I planned my departure to coincide with the march to the communion rail. I would hide out in the john until communion was over. "Better safe than sorry," I thought. "I mean, what if smoke started coming out of my mouth?"

After school that day I went over to the church hoping to run into Father Brager. Brager was a young, bald priest with a ready laugh and what I considered a somewhat liberal leaning when it came to such matters of sin, or sins of the flesh, to be exact. When I walked past the sacristy, he was just coming out.

"Hey, Father."

"How are you doing, Chuck?"

"Good. Just great, Father. Excellent, in fact. Got a minute?"

"Sure."

"I listened to your sermon today. I always listen to your sermons. They always give me lots of good stuff to think about."

"I'm sure they do."

"Anyway, that part about the mortal sins. What exactly would I need to do to commit one of those?"

Brager was smart enough to know where I was headed, having done triage on other developing Catholic minds. I could see him purse his lips and squint his eyes as he tried to resolve the theological dilemma he sensed burning within me. Finally, he said, "Well, Chuck, let me put it this way, I'd say it's virtually impossible for someone of your age to commit a mortal sin. You have my permission to take communion any time you want. How's that? Does that help you out?"

"Well, yes it does, actually. It helps me out quite a bit, Father. Thanks."

"So, how's your family?" came his quick reply as he walked with me outside the church and carried me from the issue at hand to less confusing waters.

"Oh, everything is pretty good. Everyone is doing good," I replied.

"That's the way it should be. Enjoy life, Chuck."

11.

Thrifty Pete

PETER Kisalunis was the youngest of my mother's three siblings and the only boy. He was thin framed and good looking. He had green eyes and wavy light brown hair that did not gray until well into his seventies. Like my mother he was in perpetual motion. He loved life and wore this joy on his sleeve. He was the one who could jolly my mother out of her occasional grumpy moods and he was the one who'd call my dad and say "Carl, you're coming for Thanksgiving, right?" "Carl, you are coming out the cottage, right?" "Carl, you'll let Chucky and Joey come fishing with us, right?" When my mother collapsed with what she thought was a severe heart attack, she didn't call for an ambulance, she called Pete. When life overwhelmed her, she didn't complain, she called Pete. Never for an extensive therapeutic discussion, but simply to check in and verify someone was there for her. To my mother, sorrow wasn't something you dwelt on. You took care of your business and put your faith in God, the church, and Pete.

After getting a Purple Heart as an infantryman in World War II, Pete took a job at the post office and spent the rest of his life joyfully delivering mail. Unlike Marvin, he was modulated, respectful and thrifty. He loved people and could banter with the best of them. Shooting the shit about baseball, golf, and the sale price of bratwurst at Schulz's butcher shop.

While he was a regular churchgoer, he wasn't a Holy Roller. He worked hard, but didn't put work ahead of family and fun. His life outside work was filled with fishing, camping, swimming, golfing, and sitting on the back porch and drinking a beer or a Brandy Old Fashion.

My mother had interceded to win me a day's furlough from the farm and a sleepover at my Uncle Pete's home. It was Christmas vacation. I willingly jumped into the Kisalunis soup. Their home was small like ours. It teemed with people and chores, but unlike ours, it didn't feel like a religious shrine. It gushed with joy. A sleepover at my cousin's was a trip to the other side of the world—just two miles away.

"Hey, wake up. I'm off work today. Get your pants and shoes on. We're out the door in thirty minutes." My uncle called down into the basement they'd converted into a family room where I was stretched out sleeping with my cousins, Dan and Tom. After a game of Monopoly, those of us too weak to go upstairs and crawl into a bed just fell asleep where we'd sat.

I got into Pete's ten-year-old station wagon he affectionately called Ever-ready Betty with Dan and Tom, and headed out for breakfast. I'd never had breakfast *out*. "Have I got the place for you. Great food at a great price." Pete said, as he whistled to the tune on the radio. "You know the common working man eats better than the rich most days—good wholesome food at half the price. Makes you wonder how the rich got that way with all the money they waste," he said as he turned into the small parking lot outside Hertzel's Day Old Bakery at exactly 6:55 a.m. "Kids, the early bird gets a dozen free coconut donuts. If you want the freshest day-old bakery, you got to get here ahead of the crowd. We're about to have what they call in Europe a "Continental breakfast".

"What's that?" Dan asked.

"It's pastries and coffee without bananas, eggs, and bacon. It's the breakfast all those on-the-go skinny Europeans who don't have time to cook or eat. They just squeeze their little butts into their sports cars, shovel a croissant in their mouth, and they're set for the day, or at least until lunch. When I was in southern France during the war, this is how we'd have breakfast. Just make believe you're in Paris. Think of this as your Friday morning lesson in European cuisine," Pete explained. My siblings and I loved being with him. Fishing, driving around in Betty, or sitting at the beach. It didn't matter to him that it was the same old Kingsbury beer he always drank, he'd appreciate it and enjoy every liquid drop of it. Leaning back he'd sigh, "Now, this is one great beer." Pete was the poster boy for A Great Day To Be Alive.

Ruth and Max Hertzel recognized my uncle through the front window and unlocked their store a few minutes early for one of their best customers. "Good morning, Pete. Looks like you win the dozen early bird donuts again. How many times does that make this month— six?" Max Hertzel asked. "For as much pastry as you eat, you sure look great. Must be all the walking you do delivering mail."

Max was a man who loved baked goods every bit as

much as my uncle, but suffered its calories more. Short, badly overweight, wearing white pants and shirt, with a paper hat that had *Day-Old Delights* stenciled on it, Max was yet a man in motion.

His wife, Ruth, was a perfect complement to him— tall, rail-thin, smoking one cigarette after another held in an elegant ebony cigarette holder. Like Max, she was also dressed in white, but favored slightly tinted green glasses that gave her the look of a German undercover agent in white hospital shoes. Looking at the two of them it occurred to me how couples often come in such unmatched sets. One is fat and the other is thin. One talks endlessly and the other barely says a word. One is tall and the other is short. One is earthy and the other is sophisticated.

"Peter, who's that you got with you?" Ruth asked.

"Why, this here is my nephew, Chucky Ries. Helen and Carl Ries' son. His mom got him a day pass off the farm. I'm showing him the sights and sounds of the big city," Pete said.

"Well, very pleased to meet you, Mr. Ries. How would you like a free chocolate éclair? You like chocolate éclairs, don't you?" Ruth asked, taking a drag on her cigarette and letting go of a plume of smoke that momentarily enveloped me.

"Yes, I do, Mrs. Hertzel, but I haven't had my breakfast yet." I said.

"Breakfast? That's why your uncle brought you here—no oatmeal and raisins for you. And since you're a brand new customer, I'm treating you to a free chocolate éclair. Now, you start working on this little cream-filled delight," Ruth said, munching on a powdered sugar donut and firing up a second cigarette.

"That's Ruth for you, always looking for a new recruit. Eats all day and will you take a look at her? Just as thin and beautiful as the day I married her forty years ago. And me? Every donut I touch rolls down my throat and right into my spare tire," Max laughed.

I held the chocolate éclair in my trembling hands and stared at it. Pastry and candy were relegated to Sundays only. I was caught in the crux of a sweet dilemma. Seeing the look on my face, Pete said, "Your mom said it's okay to have fun today. Go for it. Give that beauty a place to call home." With Pete's encouragement, I polished off my first chocolate éclair of the day in two bites.

"Okay kids, you can pick out six more pastries each. You can eat two now and save the rest for later. I don't want any of you getting sick when we go skiing. Hey, Max, how about a cup a coffee?" Pete said.

"Help yourself, it's right over there in our new Continental Breakfast Center I fixed up last night. I thought it would add a little European flavor to the place," Max said with pride, pointing to a small table that had cups, cream, sugar, and a fresh brewed pot of coffee on it. The French flag was tacked on the wall behind it. Pete poured a cup full, inhaled its aroma, and spent the next fifteen minutes talking with Max and Ruth, while Dan, Tom, and I finished our breakfast and picked out our to-go pieces.

Pete should have run for mayor. For I don't believe there was ever a person he didn't like and couldn't find something in common with. His capacity for joy was endless. Whether he was eating a hamburger, talking with strangers, or walking his mail route, he was someone you were glad to see. Like Marvin, you always felt fuller, happier when you were in his presence. While I didn't know how to live like this, I wanted to learn. I wanted to try. So I let myself be carried along in Pete and Marvin's stream of life. At times it felt as if I would drown or be left behind, or worse, made to realize that I would never possess such aliveness. But on another level that I could not yet realize, there was a great protecting circle forming around me when I was in the shelter of these remarkable men.

"That's it, kids. Let's get moving. If we hang around here any longer, we won't be able to squeeze our fat butts out the door," he said. We thanked our hosts, said good-bye, and walked out to the car where Pete opened the trunk and placed two grocery bags full of bread loaves, hamburger buns, hotdog rolls, and an assortment of pastries inside.

At 8:10 a.m., we were making our way to Plymouth's Municipal Ski slope, called Nut Hill. Pete wasted no time in preparing us for the next stop on our Friday tour, "Alright, kids, now listen up. We can ski for half price if we're residents of Plymouth, which we sort of are. So we need to do a little memorizing before we get there." Pete happened to have a Plymouth phone directory under his front seat and passed it back to us. "Here's your job. You three pick out a street address and memorize it. If the guy at the hill asks where you live, you tell him Plymouth, and give him the address in the book."

"But, dad, we don't live in Plymouth," Dan said from the back seat.

"Well, Dan, it's all how you look at it. My state taxes benefit Plymouth. I buy a lot of their cheese and we attend their Cheddar Days Festival. So, in a sense, we are residents of Plymouth. We just don't live there full time.

Guess that makes us seasonal residents. Sort of like those folks who live in Florida half the year. So, we're just borrowing an address for a day. How's that sound to you?"

"Oh, well, sure, if you put it like that," Dan said.

"Downhill skiing, nothing like it," Pete said as we pulled up to Nut Hill. Getting out of Betty, he surveyed the scene before him and inhaled its grandeur as if this pathetic Midwestern ski hill were the Swiss Alps. Nut Hill's incline was so gradual that skiers, even very good ones, could not exceed speeds of fifteen miles per hour. In Colorado, they would have called it a pre-bunny hill, but on this sunny, late-winter morning in Plymouth, it would be our first trip to the Alps. We were about to experience the greatest ski adventure of our lives. "Okay, guys, put on your gear. Chucky, I brought an extra pair for you. Ever been skiing? Well, it doesn't matter. Other than golf, it's the greatest sport ever created by God." Pushing me from behind, Pete took me to the bottom of the lift, "Grab hold of this towrope, let it pull you to the top of the hill, get yourself turned around, and push off. The hill will do the rest of the work for you. If you fall, get up and do it all over again," Pete said.

The four newest residents of Plymouth and four hundred other unfashionable ski bunnies went up and down the hill all day. After three hours, I was starting to understand the fundamentals of turning and stopping. It was fun, and at noon we broke for lunch. "Kids, take your skis off and come on over to the car. I have lunch ready for you." Pete had pulled out a two-foot long summer sausage, a pound of cheddar cheese, and four cans of Jolly Good Soda. From one of the Day-Old Delights bags in his trunk, he grabbed a few hamburger buns and there, in the Nut Hill parking lot, we had sausage and cheese sandwiches—the staple of any road trip meal with Pete. "So, how do you like it so far, Chucky?"

"It's great. Skiing is fun," I said.

"Well, always nice to have you along. A guy like you works hard; he should play hard. You're a natural skier. I would have thought you'd been up and down a few ski hills before today from the way you're getting around out there," Pete said.

By late afternoon we called it quits. We removed our skis and headed back to Sheboygan. "Boys, I'm starved. Let's say we get a fish fry at the Veterans of Foreign Wars Clubhouse."

Friday night Fish Fry is a Wisconsin institution. Any bar, VFW, restaurant or church basement with a deep fryer put a sign out front and invited you in. Usually you'd get five breaded, deep-fried lake perch, a cup of cole slaw, French fries, two buttered pieces of rye bread, and a beverage for five dollars. A good eat at a great price.

Ruby's VFW was just down the street from Pete's house. The seventy and over early eaters began arriving at 4:00 p.m. and by 6:00 p.m. the place was packed. Ruby Wattkowski, a full-figured woman who liked to wear her peroxide-blonde hair *big*, had managed the local VFW for the past ten years. She'd turned a place where guys sat on their barstools all day and ate hamburgers and fries into a community hot spot. It was where mom, dad, grandparents and the kids went on Friday after work to celebrate the start of the weekend. Food was served on paper plates, and if you paid eight dollars you were entitled to unlimited refills. The All-You-Can-Eat professionals were designated by an ink stamp on the back of their right hand in the image of a jumping lake perch.

Unlimited refills are risky business in a town where value eating is in vogue and in a state reputed to have the largest per capita number of fat people in the United States. But Ruby had figured that by not skimping on the quality of her lake perch *and* double-dipping them in fry batter, she had what all Wisconsinites loved— great fish at a cheap price with a thick crust. She saw the future of deep-frying. Before deep-frying cheddar balls, stuffed jalapenos, and cheddar-covered onion rings became popular, Ruby was serving them at the VFW. She had instincts for what the public wanted and she wasn't ashamed to shovel it into them. She convinced the board of the VFW to invest in a state-of-the-art deep fryer. A tight-fisted group of patriots, not thought to part with two hundred dollars for a fancy bit of cooking equipment, they let Ruby lead them down the deep fried path. And if it took a little bit of lipstick and shorter skirt than usual to get them to agree to spend the money, she didn't care. It was just good business.

Ruby's deep fry technology could have easily been duplicated. And other restaurateurs could have tacked on a few more bucks for refills or double dipped their cheddar balls, but only she could guarantee you Allen Zimmerman and His South Side Polka Rascals.

The portable marquee outside the VFW proudly blinked *Double Deep Fried Fish and The Southside Polka Rascals on Tap*. Some thought the only reason Ruby dated Allen Zimmerman, the lead singer and accordion player for the Rascals, was to make sure his band didn't work any of the other fries around town.

The Rascals all wore matching Hawaiian shirts.

The costuming was Ruby's idea. Again her marketing instincts were inspired. She sensed that melding polka with a modern tropical look would strike exactly the right balance between the older and younger generations of polka lovers. She made papier-mâché palm trees and painted a few islands floating on a blue Pacific Ocean as a backdrop. To the VFW crowd, it was like having Hawaii's favorite sons of polka play for them.

Once the seventy-and-over crowd had gone home to an early bed, the sixty-five-and-under crowd came to life. Warming up at the bar with a few beers and Brandy Old Fashions, the locals would hunker down to plates of fried fish and gaze out over a sea of grandmas dancing with daughters, moms dancing with their kids, kids dancing with kids, and husbands dancing with wives. You didn't have to be a brain surgeon to dance the polka and, indeed, I never saw many brain surgeons at the VFW.

"Hey, hey, hey, we're in luck! The Southside Polka Rascals are playing," Pete said.

"They play *every* Friday, Dad," Tom said as we got out of the car.

"Well, who cares, they're darn fine, and with Ruby's all-you-can-eat fish fry, it's great dinner entertainment," Pete said as he walked ahead of us and into the VFW.

"Hey, Ruby, got room for four more? We're so hungry we could eat a horse," Pete said just inside the front door.

"You bet, Pete, how about a seat right next to the bar with a good view of the dance floor. Ole' Allen is in rare form tonight. Thank God he gave up that stupid electric guitar. You know it's all about finding your special gift in life and some guys couldn't find it if landed on top of their head. So I helped him out. Seems to have made him happy. Just look at that big show-off," Ruby said.

"He's pretty good, Ruby. Looks like you've got another full house. You must be making some good bucks. Boys, what are you having to drink?" Pete asked.

"Well, I'm not driving a Cadillac yet, but it's paying the bills," Ruby said as we gave her our drink orders and she went off to get our meals.

The VFW had a small stage and dance floor with tables set around it. There was a large bar at the rear and a kitchen off to the right. The room was paneled in dark-stained cedar with plenty of mounted trophies on the wall—each a tribute to Wisconsin's endless hunting and fishing opportunities. There were Large Mouth Bass, Musky, Northern Pike Sturgeon, pheasant, deer, rabbit, and a lone moose who must have crossed the Wisconsin state line and gotten shot by one of our state's erstwhile headhunters.

"Hey, how's the hardest working kid in Sheboygan?" came a voice from the end of the bar.

"Hello, Mr. Heinmeister," I said.

"We got a boatload of chubs in yesterday. Tell your dad the price has never been better," Leon said as he hoisted himself off his barstool and walked over to our table.

"I will. This is my Uncle Pete and my cousins, Dan and Tom. I see you've got your lucky hat on tonight. You figuring on shooting a few bucks or something?"

"A hunter is always prepared. I never leave home without it. It's like an old friend. So, what brings you guys out on this fine Friday evening?"

"We were downhill skiing at Nut Hill all day and my uncle said he needed his fix of deep-fried fish."

"Downhill skiing. Pretty fancy. Me, I prefer to enjoy my snow with my rump in the seat of a snowmobile and a bottle of peppermint Schnapps tucked into my vest pocket."

"Are you Andy Heinmeister's brother?" my uncle asked.

"You bet I am. How do you know Andy?"

"I usher with him at the 10:15 a. m. mass on Sundays at St. Peter Claver. Nice guy. You could be his twin, except his beard is a little shorter than yours," Pete said.

"And I'm better looking, right? I thought you looked familiar. I get over to St. Pete's every now and again. I'm not an every-Sunday kind of Catholic, if you know what I mean. But I know where to find God when I need Him. I do a lot of my praying in deer and duck blinds or sitting over ice holes. Nothing like nature to bring a person close to the Lord—nature and the Green Bay Packers, that is," Leon said with a laugh.

"Well, if it isn't a Ries boy," I heard a woman's voice say from behind me. I turned to see Lilac Rummelfinger, looking as neat and tidy as ever sitting just a table over. She'd come to the VFW with her son and two of his kids. I smiled and waved hello, hoping this would keep her at her table. But Lilac took my friendly gesture as an invitation to come over and get a closer look at one of the Ries Wonders of the World.

"Hello, Pete. These must be two of your boys," Lilac said without taking her eye off me.

"That's right, Lilac. This is Tom and Dan," Pete said.

"I see you've brought your nephew with you. He comes from a very lucky family. God certainly looks with favor on the Rieses. Don't you think?"

"I guess. But we're all pretty lucky if you ask me," Pete replied.

"That orange cap Mr. Heinmeister's wearing makes him lucky, Mrs. Rummelfinger," I said. "Maybe he'd loan it to you for a week and see what happens. What do you say, Mr. Heinmeister?"

Leon took this opening and introduced himself, "Hello Lilac, I'm Chuck's chubby buddy, Leon Heinmeister—pleased to meet you."

"Well, nice to meet you, Mr. Heinmeister. So, you're a friend of the Ries family? How would they know you? Can't be from church. I don't see you around church. Are you a church man, Mr. Heinmeister?" Lilac asked, studying Leon like a novelty in a gift shop.

"I don't exactly know them from church, I know them from the docks. I'm a fisherman and a master hunter. I'm sort of Chuck's Dutch uncle. I give him little nuggets of wisdom when he comes down to the dock with his dad to get chubs. Tips every young fella needs to know. Don't I, Chuck?" Leon asked.

"That's right, Mrs. Rummelfinger. He taught me the Fisherman's cheer and how to outsmart a raging buck during deer season. See that cap," I said, pointing to Leon. "That's a deer magnet. They can't resist it. Well, one day when Mr. Heinmeister was hunting this huge buck, which was more like a Brahma bull, it came running after him and…"

"Whoa, there little chub buddy, I'm sure a nice lady

like Mrs. Rummelfinger doesn't need to hear that old hunting story," Leon telegraphed me a look that suggested he'd rather me not pursue this line of storytelling right now.

I was surprised to see how cleaned up Leon could get. He wore a slightly too small green flannel hunting shirt and a pair of corduroy pants. His beard was combed. He'd even bothered to scent himself with Old Spice after-shave. Yet despite his best attempt to remake himself in to a Friday Fish Fry chick-magnet, it appeared his clothes might explode off him in any minute, for as Leon grew, his wardrobe surely didn't.

Lilac was fifteen years Leon's senior, but hardly looked it. They were a study in contrasts. *Something is happening here.* I thought. *Leon's being rather subdued. He can rattle on for ten minutes without taking a breath of air and now he's acting like a guy running for elected office.*

Lilac also seemed a bit distracted. She was no longer staring at me, but in Leon's general direction. She wasn't exactly looking *at* him, but rather around him as if she were measuring his aura or trying to remember where she put something on the invisible shelves that were just behind him.

The Rascals had finished a polka version of Wayne

Newton's *Red Roses For a Blue Lady* and people were returning to their tables as Allen introduced the next song. The place was full and there was a comfortable din throughout the VFW when Leon asked, "Lilac, do you polka?" Lilac continued to look in his general direction, still having not yet found what she was looking for and apparently didn't hear his question. "You might not know this, but I won first place two years ago in the Sturgeon Bay Deer Hunter's Polka Fest. I'm pretty light on my feet for a biggish guy. Deer hunting and polka dancing have a lot in common. Most people don't even know that."

"I certainly didn't know that deer hunting and the polka have anything in common, Mr. Heinmeister, and I've lived in Wisconsin my entire life. But yes, actually, I do polka. Why?"

"Well, how about it? How about taking a spin with Leon?"

"Lilac, I'll say a prayer to St. Bernard the patron saint of polkas," my uncle jumped in. "Just be sure Leon doesn't step on your foot. I hear the last person he danced with is still wearing a cast."

"I'll take you up on that prayer, Pete. I haven't called on St. Bernard in awhile, but now seems like as good a time as any," Lilac said, warming to the banter. "Mr.

Heinmeister, I've never danced with a man wearing an orange hunting cap before. You can dance without it can't you? Or does it make your feet lucky too?"

"Why, what the heck, I forgot I had it on. I can dance just fine without it. Hey, little buddy, you want to guard ole' Lucky Bucky while we give it a go?" Leon said as he put the cap on my head.

After a long swelling accordion solo, the Rascals jumped into *The Tear Drop of Beer Polka* and Leon and Lilac disappeared into a sea of hop-stepping dancers. After they'd completed their first loop around the dance floor it was evident that two old pros were doing their thing and, out of respect, most the other dancers sat this one out. Turning, skipping, and changing direction under the disco ball, Leon and Lilac were two people in harmony. I saw a bumbling chatterbox and stiff church lady melt before my eyes. I didn't recognize either of them as the people I thought I knew. I considered that maybe my father was right about the truth of a person being on the inside where we can't see it. Dancing made Lilac and Leon different. She began to smile and I sensed a very small uncontrollable bubble of joy rising up in her as she and Leon whirled around the floor.

"This must be heaven. Great food, wonderful people,

super music, and you three guys. What could be better than this?" Pete said, as he put his arm around my shoulder and gave it a squeeze.

I wasn't sure if, indeed, this was heaven, but it was familiar. It was Friday Fish Fry with my Uncle Pete. As the music came to the end, Lilac and Leon circled one more time before gliding to a landing a few feet from our table and reluctantly joined the rest of us at the VFW. They were human again. Their wings would remain on the dance floor. "I don't think I have ever danced with anyone who cuts the rug as good as you, Lilac. You dance really well," Leon said.

"Well, thank you, Mr. Heinmeister, it was a pleasure to dance with you as well. You must be quite a deer hunter. I hope I see you at mass a little more often," she said and returned to her son's table, not looking back, but still trying to understand why Leon seemed so familiar to her.

"Geez, that lady can dance," Leon said as he walked over to our table and grabbed Lucky Bucky off my head. "And don't you tell me this hat ain't lucky."

12.

Dad Drives

I WAS a mediocre basketball player in grade school. If it weren't for the fact that I reached my current height of five feet eleven inches at forteen, I would never have played at all. After my first season of seventh grade basketball and, despite my failings at baseball, I was determined to remake myself into a great athlete. I shot hoops all summer. I ran laps around the mink yard. I lifted the weights Jim used to prepare himself for high school football. When my farm chores ended, my training regimen began. As always, I was tireless in my pursuit of perfection.

But despite long hours spent in athletic self-improvement, I seemed to get no better. I didn't get a lot of help from my parents. Sport camps were out of the question. I didn't know there were such things, and even if I did, I would have had to overcome my parents' long-standing self-improvement philosophy, which said, "If you're not good at something, you weren't meant to do it." They believed that real basketball players just hopped out of the womb hitting jump shots. So the chances of my getting them to spend money for someone to teach me how to play a sport were pretty slim. When it came to athletics, I was on my own.

I don't know many farm kids who have gone on to become great athletes. Those who do, most often do it in the brawn-over-brain sports of football, wrestling, pig throwing, or cow pie tossing. Those big-hearted, thick-headed plow jockeys make great linemen, but when it comes to finesse sports like basketball, golf, tennis, or soccer, forget it. That's not to say a farm kid couldn't become a great golfer, but who has time to practice? Most farmers believed as my father did—that chores and schoolwork came first. Athletics were for city kids who had nothing to do. However, practice time notwith-standing, I just didn't come into this world with natural athletic grace and nerves of steel. And to top it all off, I suffered from a chronically busy mind.

My city friends didn't seem to have this problem. They didn't worry about good versus evil or why God made them or how to serve the Lord in this world. They didn't spend time wondering whether they'd just committed a venial sin or not. They just lived and shot buckets, read *Mad* magazine, farted, and enjoyed life. So even *if* my physical attributes had been better developed, I was not psychologically designed for the pressure of competitive sports. As I stood on the free throw line with ten seconds left to play, the crowd screaming and the score tied 34 to 34, my veins did not pump ice water, nor was my mind a tranquil sea. On the contrary, my mind told me to flee and run for cover. It told me I was a pretender and would fail. On cue, I would choke and crumble under the pressure. My hands would tremble, and my mind would become a symphony of self-doubt. But, as I said, I was tall and I played. It didn't matter to me that I never scored. I enjoyed playing with my friends. It got me off the farm.

As a team, we were good. Not because we had the best players in our league, but because we had the oldest. Most of the guys on my team were the same academic underachievers who welcomed me in first grade. Some of us had already begun to grow facial hair. We had a steely competitive edge that most of our adversaries lacked. We were, after all, almost men.

Most of our games were played in Sheboygan against other local Catholic grade school teams. My mother or father would usually drop me off at these games, and I would find a ride home with one of my buddies' parents or just walk the three or four miles back to our farm. Out-of-town games demanded carpooling, however. For each of these games, there were always a few fathers who would volunteer to drive. I remember these road trips fondly—the roughhousing in the car, stopping for a hamburger and shake, and generally having a great time bonding with my fellow teammates.

Throughout my limited athletic career, I don't recall my father ever coming to a game or offering to drive as part of the carpool. He was usually too busy with farm or church work. I didn't find his absence odd. For the most part, I was coming to believe that my father didn't really exist. So I was shocked the day he volunteered to drive a bunch of my teammates to a game twenty miles from Sheboygan in Plymouth.

Being a perennial optimist, I thought this a wonderful gesture and a great opportunity for me to show my buddies that my father wasn't the dull Holy Roller they all thought him to be, but actually a fun-loving guy. Of course, I had no actual proof of this, but I still carried a glimmer of hope that given the right opportunity, his mischievous inner child would shine through, and the entire world would see that my father was not just a Type-A workaholic, but one hell of a lot of fun. He just needed a chance to prove it.

When we pulled up onto the asphalt playground that was next to the grade school, I was in high spirits. It was mid-afternoon on a Sunday in early January. The other two dads had already arrived and were seated in their cars with four of my eleven teammates in each. The remaining three hopped into the backseat of our car, and in no time we were off to Plymouth. We were optimistic about our chances of winning the game that day since we were going to be playing against a bunch of farm boys. It never occurred to me, as I joined in the taunts and laughs about the other team, that I too was just a farm boy. Maybe I thought mink farmers were a breed apart. We put fur on the backs of the fashion elite, not just chunks of cheddar cheese on the table.

The usual jousting, kidding, and punching started as soon as everyone was in the car. In a preteen reflex action, I turned the radio dial to WOKY, the local rock 'n roll and away from my father's preferred polka show. A sense of foreboding flooded over me when a few miles into our journey, my father turned the radio off. And then he did the unthinkable. He asked the assembled group, "Who'd like to say the rosary?"

Of course, no one answered. Not even Steve Mauer who later did a short stint in the seminary. I mean, *say the rosary on the way to a basketball game?! What planet was he from?!* My father took our stunned silence as a vote of confidence and said, "Okay, men. Use your fingers to keep count of the Hail Marys and Holy Marys and I'll do the rest."

I could feel three sets of eyes begin to burn holes in me from the backseat. My embarrassment made me break out into a sweat as the rosary began. Radio silence. Sitting still. Counting with our fingers while making our way to the basketball game.

I was mortified and humiliated. This was the last straw. I would disown him. *How could he do this to me?* I thought. *This can't be my real father. He can't be anyone's father;* I contemplated between Hail Marys and Holy Marys. *Please make this man disappear. Send me my real father. Oh God, if You truly exist, please save me!* But it was to no avail. Once again, God had chosen to ignore my prayer for help—a pattern I was beginning to have serious theological suspicions about. The rosary went on for the next fifteen minutes and ended mercifully when we arrived at St. Joseph's gym in Plymouth.

My friends could not get out of the car fast enough. In fact the car had not come to a complete stop when the mass exodus began. They left me sitting alone next to my father, the rear car doors wide open and a winter breeze blowing through the wind tunnel created by their rapid departure. My father placed his rosary back in its leather carrying pouch and said, "So there. That was good. Now let's get going."

Good? Yes, I guess the rosary was good for my father, but for me, on this day of days, it was just another thorn in my crown. I was defeated. I would never rise from the dead. But what could I do? I was convicted as charged of being Carl Ries' son. I accompanied his holiness into the gym and our scheduled game against the St. Joe's Panthers. I sucked it up. I focused on the game and tried to take my frustrations out on the team we called the Cheese Puffs.

We played valiantly. We should have won. We always did. Yet despite the blessings and angelic rewards our rosary should have showered upon us, we were barely beaten by a bunch of guys who knew more about milking cows than handling basketballs. Maybe all those Blessed is the Fruit of Thy Womb, Jesus' and Glory Be to the Fathers had thrown our concentration off, softened our aggressive competitive edge. Whatever it was, we lost, and the Blessed Virgin Mary didn't come to our rescue.

After the game was over, we put our heavy jackets, gloves, and galoshes back on and headed out the door to the cars that would take us home. However, unlike the excitement that marked our departure, there was now a sense of foreboding. The teammates who'd flown into my father's car before heading to Plymouth were now avoiding it. It had become infected with sanctifying grace. They were not about to re-enter my father's car or the church on wheels as it came to be known. Instead they packed themselves shoulder to shoulder in the other two cars. They didn't seem to care about bodily injury or lack of oxygen. They just wanted to be free to sing and yell and talk about the game. As for me, my fate was sealed. I crawled into the front seat of my father's car and we commenced the long silent ride home.

As I look back on that day, I marvel at how oblivious my father was to the world around him. He didn't notice feelings or the looks in people's faces. Unless his wife or children hit him over the head with a two-by-four-sized emotional crisis, he floated in a perfectly ordered world of work and routines. It didn't bother him that no one wanted to ride home with us that day. Nor did he sense my utter disappointment and embarrassment. He had no clue what had just taken place, and he didn't care. He just opened his little leather rosary case and we began another round for the salvation of saints and the forgiveness of sinners.

13.

Eight Quarts of Milk

ANOTHER breeding season had begun, and with it came the varieties of weather typical of Wisconsin in early spring. Some days it rained, some days it snowed, and some days it both rained and snowed. We dressed to stay warm and dry as we lugged breeding males from pen to pen waiting for the pairings to be completed. In those days there were no insulated boots or snowmobile suits, so we wore buckled boots and two layers of pants under our bib overalls. We called these our "work clothes" as differentiated from our "school clothes," "play clothes," and "church clothes." "Work clothes" consisted of ratty, worn, and patched jeans, flannel shirts, wool caps, denim jackets, and bib overalls that, over the course of a week, would take on the smells and colors of our farm. In the winter, the goal was to wear as many layers as possible. We even wore two layers of mittens.

It was late Saturday afternoon and four inches of snow had fallen. My three brothers and I were working various jobs. As the day drew to a close, Marvin, Jim, and I were standing at the north end of the mink yard that faced my grandfather's barn. As he bantered with my brother, Marvin mindlessly bent over and packed himself a good-sized snowball. He let it fly, hoping it would clear the top of the barn just to see if he could do it. My brother and I watched it sail over. The bait had been set. Another Life Skills Development Class was about to begin.

"Did you see that baby fly? Man, it must have gone four hundred feet! Quite a toss, don't you think, Jimmy?" Marvin said, as he proudly gazed off in the direction of his throw.

"Anyone could do that. It's no big deal," my older brother, who was fourteen at the time, snorted, doing his best I'm-a-man-already impersonation.

Setting the bait for these outdoor seminars wasn't too complicated. We were male, and while we were half the size of Marvin, our egos knew no bounds. Life had not yet taught us there were some mountains that were just too high to climb. Marvin seized upon this flaw in our natures—the distance between what we could do and what we thought we could do—and created learning opportunities to bring perspective into our dimly lit minds.

Marvin packed another snowball and let it soar. Again it flew over the barn like a Babe Ruth home run flying out of Yankee stadium. "I could do that all day long," he said. "It's amazing isn't it, Jimmy? I work all day and I work all night, and I still have enough strength to toss a snowball a mile," he continued as he gazed into the distance as if he'd just thrown a shutout in the World Series, all the while waiting for the pee-wee leaguer standing next to him to take a swing. True to every bone in his body, Jim swung.

"I could do that. Shit, anyone could do that. How much do you want to bet I can do that? How much do you want to bet that I can clear the barn roof just like you did?" came Jim's puffed-up reply.

Marvin pondered this challenge for a moment before coming up with a wager that would be fair and affordable. "How about a quart of chocolate milk?"

"No problem. No sweat. No big deal," Jim replied, displaying an amazing degree of overconfidence considering he didn't have a clue whether or not he could throw a snowball *that* far. But such is the effect of freshly minted testosterone on the young male. Under its influence, the male does not calculate with logic or reason, but rather rushes headlong into battle. He does not size up his opponent—or even look at his opponent, for that matter. He just swings. Among older, wiser males, it's called having balls that are bigger than your brains.

Jim reached his bare hands into the wet, packy snow and began shaping his spherical missile. He took a long time, instinctively knowing that posturing was key to devastating the morale of the enemy. He patted and packed with such fervor you'd have thought he was pressing a lump of coal into a diamond. By this time John and Joe had come over to see what was going on. Quickly sensing the situation, they began a chorus of taunts that foretold of Marvin's imminent defeat and the ascension of young Jimmy to the alpha male position in our small club. The effect of our little Greek chorus was to swell Jim's already bloated self-confidence to helium balloon proportions. "Stand back. I'll need some room to breathe, fellas. You guys are crowding me. Let da'man have some room," he boasted while Marvin, ever the good sport and consummate contestant, stepped back to make room for Mighty Mouse. With that Jim let it fly and it struck halfway up the barn roof. "Shit, shit, shit! I can't believe it. Bad throw. I almost made it. I must have gripped it wrong. I should have ripped the roof off with that one. Well, that won't happen again, believe you me! Okay, old man, your turn."

As Marvin prepared another snowball, he did his best wide-eyed innocent impersonation. "Wow, Jimmy! I had no idea you could toss a snowball that far. It almost went over the barn. You've got quite an arm for a little squirt. Okay, it's my turn." He proudly sent another one sailing over, and then proclaimed the score, "Ole' Marvelous: ONE, and Li'l Jimmy: ZERO."

A shadow fell over my brother's face and a brooding determination came welling up. Like a man at the craps table who knew his luck was about to change, he bet Marvin another quart of chocolate milk. Jim never gave a moment's thought as to how he would pay, since losing was not one of the options presented him by his under-developed cerebral cortex.

With the Chorus chanting taunts and singing praise in the background, Jim again began preparations to unseat the champ and claim his rightful place in the winner's circle. Taking a short running start like an Olympian about to loft a javelin, he hurled the snowball through the air. It soared a bit farther than his previous toss, but still landed a few feet short of clearing the barn.

"Man, did you guys see that? That was so damn close!" Marvin said. "Just a couple of feet further and it would have cleared the barn. How close can you get! Maybe Mighty Mouse isn't such a pipsqueak after all. How about double or nothing?" he continued, just trying to be helpful and guide his young minion to success.

Jim didn't pause to think or even breathe before accepting the new wager.

Marvin let another one sail over the barn. Again Jim came close as he planted a snowball just a few feet from sweet victory. *Must-win, what-the-hell-is-going-on-here?* thoughts ran through my brother's overheated mind as he considered what must be some mistake of cosmic proportions. *I should be winning. It's obvious that I should be able to throw a damn snowball over a barn roof if Marvin can.* One could see his synapses beginning to misfire as he blurted out the final wager. "Okay, double or nothing. One more time. I can't believe it. This makes no sense."

My brother walked in slow, tight circles, pounding one fist into the other. He pursed his lips, focused his eyes, and gathered all his powers of concentration. The Chorus settled into a low, slow, evocative chant: "Jimmy,

Jimmy fo-fo Jimmy; throw the ice ball and show no pity!" The Chorus passed high fives all around, proud of coming up with such a clever chant on such short notice, and continued repeating the refrain while their hero prepared to pull a victory out of the jaws of certain defeat.

As he circled, Jim remembered the power the Lord can have in moments of great need and said a prayer to his patron saint, Saint James. Silently mouthing his request as he packed his snowball, Jim visualized the beatific image of Saint James standing on the top of the barn roof, beckoning his namesake's throw, and better still, guaranteeing him that it would fly high over the barn. Saint James held his saintly arms aloft in the gesture recognized the world over as touchdown. Jim was certain his Sainted Patron had come to the rescue. Goliath was going down. He, James Francis Ries, would be carried home on the shoulders of his adoring fans. Greatness was just one throw away.

Rounding his last and most holy snowball of the afternoon, Jim filled it with saving grace and all the power of the angels in heaven. Then he let it fly. It looked good. It was a great toss, a heroic effort, but it landed a few painful inches short of clearing the rooftop. There would be no joy in Riesville for Mighty Jimmy had just struck out!

Marvin bellowed with laughter and victory. "Well, junior, you owe old Uncle Marv eight quarts of chocolate milk. I'm sure looking forward to drinking *all that chocolate milk*. Yum, yum, yum. I just *love* chocolate milk," he said smacking his lips as Jim stood silently, staring at the image of his patron saint standing high atop the barn and looking down at him with the *pray harder and better luck next time* expressions saints often have when they fail to deliver on the holy goods.

As my brothers and I headed to the house for dinner, Marvin bid us a good day and reminded Jim just one more time that he was looking forward to receiving payment on their bet the following morning.

. . .

As Jim recovered from the humiliation of his defeat, it dawned on him that he had a bet to pay the next day. Since my parents had all of us on a forced savings program, we had no discretionary money. This involuntary savings system meant any of the wages we earned working for my father went directly into our savings accounts. Even if Jim had the money, he'd need a driver to take him to the grocery store to buy the milk. He was also sure his betting would not be welcome news to my parents. But feeling that he had no choice in the matter, he shared his lack of good judgment with everyone at the dinner table that evening.

"You did what?! You're fourteen years old. What are you doing making bets? Do you think money grows on trees? Just how many quarts of milk do you owe him?" my mother asked.

"Eight," came Jim's anemic reply, as the now silent Chorus looked on like vultures at a tennis match. Six hungry eyes following the volleys back and forth between Jim and our irate mother, relishing the sight of him squirming before the grand inquisitor.

"Eight!" My mother said and then went limp and silent, pursing her lips, shaking her head, and wondering what she had done to be blessed with not just five sons, but a rental son who came to work every day and corrupted her children. Equally perturbing was my father's inability, or lack of desire, to confront Marvin about these periodic infractions of proper child rearing.

"And why didn't any of you try to stop this?" she asked the co-conspirators sitting nearby. "Don't you have brains? Can't you look out for your brother? Can't you tell him to stop being so stupid!" Each of us displayed a look of complete puzzlement and wonder at her question. *You mean us? You mean we're supposed to look out for him?*

She then turned to her partner in life and said, "Well, Carl, what are you going to do about this?"

"Well, what do you want me to do?" came his standard reply. He returned his gaze to his plate of food and away from the searing look of my mother, who promptly let out an exasperated, "God's forgotten me! God help us all." She got up from the table and began to clear dishes, mumbling some inaudible appeal to St. Helen to keep her from doing harm to her family.

. . .

The next morning our beleaguered mother marched Jim out to the feed house, where she knew she would find Marvin preparing to mix the day's feed. Ever the charmer, he knew exactly why she was there and greeted her with a cheery, "Good morning, Helen. What brings you out to the feed house this fine morning?"

Holding eight quarts of milk, with Jim standing behind her, she took no time to reply, "Can't you see he doesn't use the five cents' worth of brains the good Lord gave him? Here are the eight quarts of chocolate milk he owes you. Please don't do this again." She handed him a brown Piggly Wiggly shopping bag filled with bottles of chocolate milk.

"Well, thanks, Helen. He did come close a few times, but fell just a little tiny bit short."

"I'm sure he did," my mother said and turned toward the house, feeling overwhelmingly certain that males were the inferior gender and that God had given her the job of shepherding a flock of underachieving sheep.

Outside earshot of my mother, Jim tossed a final, "I'll beat you next time. You got lucky. My patron saint let me down. The wind conditions were bad. My arm was tired." Marvin nodded affirmatively, admiring Jim's pluck and loving him all the more for it.

Jim never got used to losing to Marvin. Of my four brothers, he was the most purely prototypical male. A knucklehead like the rest of us, but convinced that the path to manhood lay in beating Marvin. He never did. Though Marvin loved him first among us all, mentored him, and always acted as his big brother, such fidelity did not translate into losing contests of skill, agility, or strength just to make Jim feel good. Marvin knew that a victory is only sweet when it is truly won.

14.

Bigger than Life

I HAD never been so close to death. Close to the kind of pain that shrinks a big man down to skin, bones, and remorseless depression. As I sat in a chair three feet from him, even I could see the sorrow that came from him and washed over me. Sorrow in a man who could not harbor sorrow because he was the joy in life. Marvin Rammer was dying of bone cancer at the age of thirty-eight. His cancer continued to spread, as radiation and chemotherapy treatments failed. Even with pain medications his suffering was overwhelming. Every part of his body ached, and unable to cure him, they brought him home to die. A hospital bed was set up in the small sitting room that was just off the living room in the home he shared with his wife, Sandy, and their four young children.

He had stopped working for my father a few years earlier, but we continued to see him during pelting, breeding, and grading seasons when extra help was needed. He'd work eight hours at a local foundry during the day and then install kitchen cabinets at night. He was the most tireless, joyful person I had ever known. A mentor who taught my three brothers and me about the life that either was unknown to my father or lay forgotten with him.

.   .   .

As I sat there, I recalled one late-July day three years earlier when Marvin, Joe, and I were removing manure from under the sheds. We hoisted pitchfork after pitchfork of it onto a manure spreader that was pulled by a small tractor. Since we were eleven and twelve years old, Joe and I would work one side of the alley that ran between the sheds, and Marvin would work the other side. Feeling cocky, we bet him we could out-shovel him. We bet him two dollars we could manure the pens on our side of the alley faster then he could his. We knew he was fast, but we weren't milquetoast and we could move plenty fast if the incentive were right. Certainly fast enough to out-shovel a thirty-five-year-old man.

Marvin hopped up on the tractor, slid it into first gear, slowly let up on the clutch, and jumped down onto his side of the wagon, allowing the tractor to roll forward at a slow, steady pace. "You guys look pretty fearsome. I'm so nervous I'm even going to give you a ten-foot head start just to show you how worried I am," he said, and the race was on. We hauled ass and tossed mink shit like two diesel-powered engines.

"You couldn't beat an old lady wearing lead boots! You've got so much hot air in you, you could float away in a fart-filled balloon!" we yelled our insults over the wagon in Marvin's direction.

"Yup, you guys are quite a team," he hollered back casually, thrusting one huge forkful of shit after another into the wagon. "Nobody's going to beat two power pooper-scoopers like you," he said as he let a big, wailing fart fly back across the wagon in our direction, cracking us up, and for a moment causing us to lose our Zen-like concentration.

"We're going to beat the old man, Joe," I said breathlessly as I shoveled and tossed. With twenty feet remaining between us and victory, Marvin stepped it into third gear.

From the corner of my eye, I could see my mother standing far up the aisle watching what she quickly surmised was yet another contest between Marvin and her sons. "You boys should know better than to race Marvin.

You never win, and he gets a full day's work out of you by noon. Come up for lunch after you've lost," she said.

We paid no mind to our mother's comments. We had a race to win. In fact, her doubts about our competitive form only fueled our furor to win. Breathless, we powered on. Marvin blew another foul flower over the wagon and began singing Johnny Cash's *Burning Ring of Fire*, all the while blazing a path to the end of the shed.

Marvin could manure sheds like John Henry could drive rail spikes. When he arrived at the final shed post, he punched his pitchfork into the ground, hopped up on the wagon to stop it, and raised his arms like Rocky Balboa, shouting, "Done, done, done, and I can't believe that I've won...again! I guess I'm not so old after all," he shouted with a laugh. My brother and I stood silent and frustrated. We'd lost, and we never would beat him. But we loved how he won. He brought joy to our defeat.

. . .

"Chuck, why don't you go see Marvin with your brother Jim?" my mother asked. "He's not going to be with us much longer. I know he'd love to see you." Jim and John would come home from Madison, where they were going to college, to help my dad with farm work and to visit Marvin. Jim was devastated. They were kindred spirits—fun loving and good-looking. Jim had brought his new girlfriend home for Marvin to meet and approve of. He'd go deer hunting with him every November and forever loved to drink and bullshit with Marv.

I'd tried not to hear the dinner table conversation about Marvin and his cancer. I felt awkward in moments of looming emotion. What do I say? What do I do? Where do I find words? Truth is, I didn't want to see him. I didn't want to see what death looked like, but here I was riding with Jim out to Marvin's small farm to pay our respects to the biggest life I had ever known as it died.

"Hey, the Ries boys are here! How are you doing, Jimmy? And you brought Chucky too! Nice of you boys to come visit. You want a beer and shot, Jimmy? How about you, Chucky, you want a soda or something?" Marvin's wife, Sandy, greeted us as we walked into the kitchen. She was a short, attractive woman with black hair, a great smile, and a kind manner that always made the Ries boys feel welcome. "He's not doing so good today, Jimmy. He's hurting pretty bad lately," Sandy went on. She and my brother talked as my mind drifted from that kitchen and that place to anywhere more comfortable. I sat at the end of the powder yellow kitchen table with matching vinyl chairs, having my soda and eating some pretzels. Another good friend of Marvin's arrived and joined in the discussion at the table. "Chucky, you want to go see Marv, don't you?" Sandy asked. "I know he'd love to see you."

I didn't want to move, but said, "Sure, I'd like that, as long as I'm not bothering him."

She motioned for me to follow her into the sitting room where Marvin lay sleeping. "He's resting. Have a seat. Spend some time with your old buddy," she whispered, rubbing my head gently with her hand and leaving me there next to him as the sun streamed though the windows on that early autumn afternoon.

I didn't recognize him. He'd become an old man, thin and yellow in color. Marvin had disappeared. The Marvin who taught us to laugh, told us about women, and gave us our first taste of beer was gone. The life of the party was dying. I wanted to get up and run, but stayed in my seat because it was the right thing to do. I couldn't look at him. He couldn't be dying. The noise and the voices from the kitchen comforted me as I looked around the room, swinging my legs forward and back, hoping he wouldn't wake up. Hoping my visit could end soon and that Sandy would come and take me back to the kitchen.

"Look who's come to visit," I heard a whisper coming from Marvin. I looked up, turning my attention from picking the dirt from under my fingernails toward the voice of the friend I'd come to see. "What are you up to, Chucky?"

"Nothing much. I just wanted to see you. Came to visit. Heard you weren't feeling well. I'm sorry Marvin, I feel...," I said as my voice cracked with a mixture of bewilderment and sorrow.

"Well, I am glad you came," he said, grimacing as the pain took a moment to rise up out of him and scream before it lay back down and gathered strength to scream again.

I felt helpless. I wanted to be doing something, getting something, anything other than just sitting there and trying to comprehend what the hell was going on. "You need anything, Marv? I can do something for you, if there's something you want me to do," I said, reaching for words to fill the silence. Struggling not to lose control.

"Shake my hand good-bye, Chucky, and crank my bed back a bit. There is a handle on the front—just turn it once around. No harder than shoveling a shed out. Marv's gotta get some sleep." I got up and cranked the bed as he told me to do. I stood next to him taking his thin cold hand in mine. Not shaking it, but holding it. Remembering all the life he'd given my brothers and me while working and competing in hundreds of dumb contests he knew we'd never win. I looked at him and through him. He gave me a tired wink and closed his eyes. His hand slipped from mine and fell back onto the bed as he drifted off to sleep. For a long moment, I stood there studying the paradox of death taking a life that was so bright and urgent. I worked hard to stop something that was rising up inside me from reaching my throat and eyes. I didn't want to be here. I turned and walked quickly to the kitchen.

As I entered, Sandy turned my way and asked, "How's your friend Marv doing?"

"Not so good. He's not so good." I replied, leaning against the doorway and keeping my gaze focused on the floor.

"He's dying, Chucky, but he lived big enough for two lifetimes, so maybe that's why he has to die so young," she sighed.

"I guess so," I replied, and returned to the end of the table to my soda and my cup of pretzels, and then drifted away.

• • •

Marvin died ten days later. I was sixteen and was half-way through my freshman year in high school. I went to the funeral with my family. During the vigil, I didn't visit his coffin. I didn't want to see him "that way." I didn't want those feelings to well up inside me again. Rieses weren't good at feelings. I sat in the back of the funeral parlor that was just a few blocks from our church and tried to make sense of it all.

There is the father we are each born to, but there are also the fathers we are given. Men who appear in our lives and magically see our nature and potential so clearly, it's as if they'd known us forever. Marvin was our friend, but he was also our father.

That night as I lay in bed, I wondered if those who light up life are also killed by it. Was my father right? Was life a dead-silent place where we work and worship? They never said it, but I often saw "that look" in my parents' eyes when Marvin got a new snowmobile, bought a horse for trail riding, or lived too big. Sure they loved him, but maybe God punishes those of us who are bigger than life. Maybe my father was right.

15.

High School

I BEGAN my freshman year in high school in 1967. While Sheboygan slept, the rest of the county was alive with controversy over civil rights, the Vietnam War, nuclear arms, the environment, drug use, sexual freedom, and nonconformity. The four-day concert in the summer of 1969 called Woodstock would herald a counterculture in full bloom. Everyone was being invited to tune in, turn on, drop out, and expand his or her consciousness. By contrast, my past eight years had been decidedly focused on limiting the extent of my enlightenment.

Like my six siblings, I was offered the seminary option. Joe followed the others and attended seminary high school, but my parents had begun to gently encourage me to stay home. Somewhere in the recesses of their minds, they wondered why all their children had left home after eighth grade. Bob and Kathleen had gone on to take their final vows, which made them official soldiers of God. Jim, John, and Sue all dropped out after a short stay in the seminary or convent and opted for the secular life. I felt stuffed with Catholicism. I'd eaten too many rosaries and had all the sanctifying grace I could stomach. I never gave my parents credit for being tuned in to me, but they must have sensed that the seminary was not for me. They proposed that I attend Sheboygan East High School. Secretly, they hoped I'd be the son to pick up the furred gauntlet and become the next Mink Master.

I struggled to fit into my new environment. I worked hard and was as earnest as ever. And while I didn't view myself as particularly smart, athletic, or handsome, I did have a gift for relating to a wide cross-section of humanity. Whether they were dairy farmers, potheads, jocks, shop kids, slow learners, or honors students, I could get along with them. In this regard, my parents had taught me well. I had learned from years of practicing invisibility around my parents that giving people what they wanted usually guaranteed they'd like you. At Sheboygan East, I was an over-achieving, pleasant, humble boy and a friend to all. Not offending and being liked and likable was everything to me.

Freshman year in high school is the great melting pot of early adolescence—the first stop on a journey toward adulthood. Kids from schools and neighborhoods all over town are thrown together to create a new social order. It's a race to find out where in the maze you fit and into what box you will be placed. Since I already knew I was unworthy, I didn't view myself as superior to anyone. I roamed far and wide and, much to my surprise, found that quiet persistence and being kind to all God's children had its rewards.

The first public acknowledgment of my populist value came the winter that my peers in the freshman class voted me their Ice Carnival King. I found fame a mixed blessing. While I tried to glow on the outside, I still stuttered on the inside. I was convinced that I was not special in any way. But the world didn't know any of this. It only sensed a common wholesome goodness. I was Everyman.

"Hi, Chuck. Congratulations on being elected Ice Carnival King. It's about time a *regular* human being got elected king. I am so sick of the Ken and Barbies around here winning everything. You'd think looks were some kind of ultimate blessing like ethics, honesty, sincerity, or intelligence. Why should we reward people for what they look like? What matters is what people are on the inside," Clara Weidemeyer said between classes. Clara was the subject of unrelenting taunts by our classmates. Her appearance became a thing of legend. A local garage band even wrote a song in her honor:

You can kiss me anytime
Clara
You're so ugly you make me blind
Clara
You've convinced me dumb is fine
Clara
You're all right
Yes, you're all right

The song continued on through six more stanzas of rhyming humiliations. Things weren't good for Clara Weidemeyer. She was butt ugly. The kind of ugly that made people who didn't know her assume she was retarded. Short and stocky, Clara had horrible acne and frizzed-out hair that bloomed on humid days into a sizable Afro—God hadn't given her much to work with. No redeeming physical attribute like great legs, a wonderful voice, or beautiful eyes. She did the best she could with the considerable intelligence she was given. She excelled in every subject. She participated in student government. She had a social conscience, but despite her heroic efforts to fit in and be accepted, she was as fragile as any girl would be with a face and body no one wanted to look at.

Knowing Clara led me to the uncharitable conclusion that a person may be better off dumb and good looking than smart and ugly. The proof of this theory was all around me.

"I told everyone I could to vote for you. You're one of us. You're a regular person," she told me one day in the hall between classes.

"Well, thanks, Clara. I'm just as surprised as anyone. I mean, I'm not a jock and I'm not a brain and I'm not one of the beautiful people. So I just figured, why even think about it? But, I think I'm pretty happy about being selected. I mean, who wouldn't be happy about it? Right?" I said, looking furtively down the corridor over her shoulder to make sure no one had spotted us. Fifteen seconds in the hall talking with Clara Weidemeyer could have serious consequences for one's social standing. I was trained to be more compassionate than most, but I wasn't blind. I wanted to slip away from Clara before I was branded Quasimodo's boyfriend. It was one thing to talk with her at student government meetings or exchange views in social studies class, but it was the kiss of death to hang with her in the hall.

"I would be honored to have a dance with you tomorrow night at the Carnival," Clara said.

"Wow. Well, thanks. I'll have to see how this whole thing plays out. I've never been a king before. It must come with certain responsibilities. So my time might be a little tight. I'm sure I'll have to do a few turns with Molly Murphy. But maybe you could help me with my math, which I am still flunking."

I wasn't sure if Clara would take the bone I'd tossed her and forget about the dance. *God, I can't believe I'm being such a coward*, I thought. *But I can't do it. I can't dance with her in public. Hell, I can barely talk with her in public. It's one thing for her to help me with my math, but dance? I can't do it.* I had told a white lie. If Clara was the epitome of ugly, Molly Murphy was the pure embodiment of beauty. Perfect skin, large round breasts, full round brown eyes, tall and thin, with hair that glistened and lips like two party invitations. Clara's ugliness and intelligence amazed me as much as Molly's beauty and vacuousness. They both left me speechless, but for very different reasons.

"Chuck, anyone in this school would be honored to

help you. You're such a nice person. You've never made fun of me. I know what I look like. I know what they say. There isn't too much I can do about it. I mean, look at me. I'm not going to be picked for the lead in the school play unless it's an eighty-year old woman. But you never joined in. You respect people, and that's why you deserve to be our King."

"Hey, Clara, maybe I'm just a good pretender," I laughed nervously while admiring her ability to just accept who she was. "I might secretly be a detestable person. In fact, I often think I am. Look, neither one of us are going to win any beauty contests, but it's like you said—there are a lot of beautiful people who don't have one original thought in their heads. They wouldn't know civil rights from civil engineering. Hey, in case you didn't notice, there're a lot more ordinary looking people in the world than there are beauty queens. So as Ice Carnival King, I do hereby declare that every day shall be *Take an Ordinary Person to Lunch Day.*"

"There. You see what I mean, that's exactly why we voted for you. You're just so darn cute and nice to people," Clara beamed at me as I headed off down the hall to safer ground. She was mistaking me for someone else and it made me nervous.

As I walked away, I patted myself on the back for putting myself into the same ordinary boat as Clara and thereby raising all ugly people to a cultural ideal. I had developed a forger's instincts and could quickly detect and become what people wanted me to be. I went wherever social acceptance blew me. But something deeper was happening. I was growing curious about people like Clara Weidemeyer. She was hard on the eyes, but her mind was unique. I was becoming a student of slackers, eccentrics, and intellectuals—kids who didn't fit in, but seemed to be uniquely themselves. I was tired of oatmeal for breakfast. I wanted more chocolate éclairs.

. . .

Friday night was the Ice Carnival. It was a simple affair held in the gym, with a band and, of course the highlight of the evening, the crowning of royalty. I was invited forward with my queen. Principal Paul Hersch draped red velvet capes over each of us and placed crowns on our heads. After the coronation, we were invited to do a spotlight dance before our subjects—just Queen Molly and King Charles. I had my arms around the most beautiful girl in the world. I smelled the strawberry scent of her shampoo and brushed up against her young firm breasts. When it happened, a predatory hard-on sprang out of nowhere. I wasn't driving this bus anymore.

Just what I need! Everyone's going to notice I got one going right here under the spotlight, I thought as I pulled my cape more tightly around me and distanced my hips from my buxom queen while still holding her tight. It was a rather gymnastics-like dance move, but hard-on or not, I wasn't going to release my grip on paradise.

I was in love with Molly Murphy. Every guy in school wanted her, but I had her. Me, the man of the moment. Me, the people's choice. We danced badly, rocking back and forth. Given my surprise visitor, we leaned into each other creating a kind of dancing pyramid. I'd prepared for this magic moment by getting an ID bracelet—the marker by which all men would know Molly was *my* woman.

As we rotated in the glow of three hundred worshipful eyes, I whispered, "Molly, will you go steady with me? Will you be my girlfriend?" Her eyes opened wide. I wasn't sure whether she was overcome with emotion at finally winning my heart or in shock that a dork like me would say these words to her. I wanted to retract my offer. I wanted to return to the practice sessions I'd been having in my head, each one ending with Molly saying, "Yes, Chuck, I will be your girlfriend forever and a day!"

But her reply was not the one I'd scripted.

"Joel Stegameyer just asked me to go steady with him yesterday. Thanks for asking. You're such a nice guy." She replied as if she were thanking me for loaning her my stapler rather than offering her my heart. It was no big deal to her. She was a pro at going steady. Hell, she had a scorecard just to keep track of all the offers. Compared to me, she was a woman of the world. A city woman being courted by a mink farmer. I was no match for the quarterback of the football team.

I hadn't realized how fleeting regal privilege could be. When the song ended, Queen Molly quickly deserted me and left me standing alone as she floated like a touchdown pass into the outstretched arms of Joel Stegameyer. Wearing my cape and crown, I walked to the punch table. My heart had been ripped out of my chest, leaving a cavernous hole. Of course, it didn't take much in those days—young love came and went so quickly and so painfully. At the punch table I reached up for one of the two royal goblets that were set atop a fake ice pedestal for the King and Queen to drink from after their coronation dance, and ladled myself a cupful.

"Chuck, I want to dance with you a bunch. Come on, let's dance." I heard a raspy voice from behind me say.

I froze. I knew who it was. "Hello there, King Charles," she sang to get my attention. "Would you like to dance with one of your subjects?" I heard the voice speak to me again.

How bad could it get? First being denied by Molly Murphy and now being sought by Clara Weidemeyer. Heaven and hell were next-door neighbors tonight. My balls tightened up under me. The remnant of the stiffy I'd gotten in anticipation of claiming the fair young maiden Molly was now limp and racing after my balls in a hasty retreat. "Oh, it's you, Clara. What was that you said…you want some *punch*?"

"Close. I said, 'I'd like to dance with you a *bunch*.'"

I had no choice. It was the right thing do. I did the pity dance. I danced like the cornered, equal opportunity rat-fink that I was. I heard the occasional "woof woof woof" or the little too loud "I think I'm going to throw up" as we circled the dance floor. I was raised to feed the poor and dance with the lepers, and so I did.

"So, how's it being king for a day?" Clara asked.

I didn't want to tell her that I thought it sucked and that this kind of honor was better bestowed on beautiful people who don't need a single original idea in their heads to be happy. I couldn't tell her the truth. She thought my achievement was what it must feel like to be popular. I was her representative among the ruling elite. The one she had personally canvassed to get elected. How could I step on her dream? I didn't want to let her know I wasn't special. The truth was, I wanted acceptance just as much as she did.

Awards continued to find their way to me, and I struggled to balance them. I had been well schooled and knew disaster was the flip side of every success. And didn't vanity proceed the fall? Wasn't Wile E. Coyote smashed flat as a pancake just as he thought he'd captured the elusive and succulent Road Runner? My mother's constant admonitions that I was not special were now firmly rooted in my mind. I was scaling Mount Everest with a bowling ball attached to one leg. It could be done, but the process would be painfully slow.

. . .

"Boys and girls, next Monday we begin our section on poetry," my freshman English teacher, Mrs. Mary Werner, said. "Poetry is the art of choosing words carefully to express your deepest thoughts and feelings. In poetry we use common words for uncommon purposes. To begin our section, I want each of you to bring a poem to read to your classmates next Monday. It can be any poem you like, but it has to be a poem, not a song lyric. Try to find something nice, something that speaks to your soul," she went on.

Like most of my classmates, I took the path of least resistance and looked around the house for a book with a poem in it. Since I knew no one but my brother Bob would have a book of poetry, I headed to the room he used when he visited on the weekends or stayed during summer vacations. I searched the bookshelf and found a small paperback called *A Coney Island of the Mind* by a poet named Lawrence Ferlinghetti. Ferlinghetti was one of the founding fathers of the Beat Generation. It was he who published Allen Ginsberg's seminal poem *Howl*. But all of that was of no concern to me; I was just looking for a quick fix to a class assignment.

Bob left for the seminary when I was two years old. When I was entering the fifth grade, he was entering graduate school. He was a tall, scrawny guy with big ears, a high forehead, wispy hair, and owlish glasses. He would come home a few weekends a month and bring class-mates from the seminary with him. They were a lively, entertaining group—intelligent, articulate, and devoted to social justice. On the Friday and Saturday nights they visited, I would go to school at the dinner table.

"Six thousand people marched down Wisconsin

Avenue yesterday. It's so wrong what they're doing in Vietnam. It's a horror. I can't believe more members of the church aren't speaking up about it. Sometimes I think our church fathers are just as much a part of the problem as our elected officials. What a crime," Bob said.

"Mike and six of his friends were arrested yesterday for burning draft files. It's shaking a lot of people up. Bob, it's going to take time," Sal Green, one of Bob's classmates, said.

"Slow, steady commitment is what it takes. I can't believe our government would condone this sort of thing. LBJ must be a captive of the conservative right. What's got into him?" Dan O'Brien chimed in.

I listened as they talked about acts of civil disobedience to protest the Vietnam War or efforts to integrate Milwaukee. I listened as they talked of an interpretive Bible. A Good Book where stories and parables weren't meant to be taken literally, but viewed as metaphors. I learned that the Red Sea didn't actually open and let the Jews pass through. I learned that manna didn't fall from heaven, and of course, if all this was true then maybe Jesus didn't rise from the dead, and maybe Mary wasn't a virgin, and maybe Jesus wasn't God, and maybe lying once in awhile was okay, and maybe masturbating every night wouldn't make me go blind. I was incrementally becoming a very liberal Catholic.

The adolescent mind is a sponge without prejudice or censorship. It's a mind that can still believe there are monsters under the bed and that dreams come true. It's a mind where love and devotion are uncomplicated. Ideas planted in this mind grow to become the menu from which we select what we love and what our life's work will be. If we were wiser, we'd take every nine, ten, and eleven year-old and give them a single teacher whose job it is to guide them incrementally toward themselves. Bob was, without knowing it, awakening me to parts of my deeper nature—the activist, the artist, and the mystic.

As I flipped through Ferlinghetti's book of poems, I came across one titled "Christ Climbed Down." I thought it was an accessible poem, one that my class-mates would enjoy.

The following Monday, my classmates and I suffered through the reading of thirty poems. When my turn came, I got to my feet, carried my small, odd book to the front of the class, and read aloud. As I rounded the corner into the final stanzas, I poured it on:

> *Christ climbed down*
> *from his bare tree*

this year
and ran away to where
no fat handshaking stranger
in a red flannel suit
and a fake white beard
went around passing himself off
as some sort of North Pole Saint
crossing the desert to Bethlehem
Pennsylvania
in a Volkswagen sled
drawn by rollicking Adirondack reindeer
with German names
and bearing sacks of Humble Gifts
from Saks Fifth Avenue
for everybody's imagined Christ child
...Immaculate Reconception
the very craziest
of second Comings.

I raced to the finish and looked up triumphantly over a sea of blank faces. Faces that didn't understand why they were puzzled. Faces that were not quite sure what they had just heard, but were happy to applaud the best effort of their classmate and friend.

"Well, Chuck, that was nice. Thank you for sharing

such an interesting poem. Where did you find a poem like *that*?" my instructor asked.

Ms. Werner was a woman in her mid-fifties with a decided leaning toward Emily Dickinson and T.S. Eliot. She made all her own clothes and tended her herb garden on weekends. She had never heard of Lawrence Ferlinghetti, and the only beats she ever knew she put into her beet soup.

"Well, it's about Christ coming down from the cross and seeing what a mess our society is in. I suppose the poet is telling us he can't stand stupid Bible salesmen, or fat handshaking strangers in red flannel suits who think they're some sort of *North Pole Saint*. Isn't that funny—a North Pole Saint." I laughed out loud, shaking my head and raising my eyebrows, amazed that any mind could put such seemingly unrelated ideas and concepts all in one place. "I never would have thought of Santa Claus as a saint, would you, Mrs. Werner? Wow, Mr. Ferlinghetti has quite a strange mind. Don't you think?" I responded proudly. Emboldened and feeling full of myself, I proceeded to let my mind wander further afield.

"Christ figures that it's better hanging on the cross than living in today's world and so He decides to just crawl back into his mom's womb. *Immaculate Reconception*, don't you love that?" I laughed again. "Phew, what a crazy mind!"

"Well. Okay. That was very interesting, Chuck. Mr. Ferlinghetti is quite a writer, but I don't think this is the sort of poetry most people like. Does anyone have a question for Chuck?" Ms. Werner concluded, ignoring the two waving hands as she moved from her chair in the back of the room to the front of the class. She further doused my literary fire with a good, rousing bucketful of love poetry by Elizabeth Browning.

It was dawning on me that when it came to art, religion, and social activism, my brother Bob was a bit further afield than I had imagined. Since every idea was fair game at the dinner table, it hadn't occurred to me that *some* ideas weren't meant for public consumption. Yet, it was these very ideas that drew me. I didn't know Ferlinghetti was strange or that my brother was odd. To me, he was big city. He lived among people who drank issues and beauty and justice. His books, his art, and his ideas were leading me to a part of myself that was slowly stirring. The city lights were going on.

16.

The Lesson

MY MOTHER'S ability to guard me against my
deepest desires was brought into sharpest relief after I
experienced a minor triumph. I discovered I had some
talent as an actor. Acting allowed me to pretend to be
someone else. It was a momentary cure for my burning
brain, and it gave me a time-out from being perfect and
guilty and Ries.

After performing in a few smaller roles, I was cast to
play the lead in *The Lesson* by Eugene Ionesco. Ionesco is
the father of the theater of the absurd. He wrote a number
of plays in which language is reduced to a bantering
game where words obfuscate rather than elucidate the
truth. *The Lesson* is a masterpiece of crazed, confused,

and irrational language. In it a professor (played by me) uses language to symbolically kill his student—in this case a cute airhead who represents society. In this thirty-minute one-act play, the student is bombarded with language that deteriorates into mad word volleys. I had what amounted to twenty pages of illogical monologue to memorize. This was no job for a weak-kneed, candy-ass actor. At any age, it would take real concentration just to memorize the lines and some degree of talent to perform them. But *talent* was not something I was aware of possessing. Due to my mother's vigilance in making sure we'd never be too big for our britches, I thought I was quite ordinary. Yet, within me burned a flame that wanted to be extraordinary.

Despite the challenges of this play, I was brilliant. During the standing ovation, I saw that my parents remained seated. Their quandary over my success would deepen the following day when the Sheboygan Press gave me a rave review. Okay, so it was just a high school play. So what!

As I floated in the front door of our house after the opening performance, filled with the fresh glow of my theatrical breakthrough, she was sitting there waiting with her silent acolyte, my father, standing at her side.

As one might expect, I was filled with the kind of uncluttered, spontaneous pride that boosts young teens when they believe they have conquered the world. When they believe they have just discovered what God created them for. "Wasn't I great? Wasn't I amazing? I mean, a standing ovation! I wasn't expecting that. I didn't blow a single line. God, that felt great. Hey, maybe I could study acting in college, go on to Broadway, and become famous! Famous? I could get into that." I rattled on as I stuck my head into the refrigerator.

"What makes you think you're so special?" my mother said, sounding like the Great Oz. *What makes me think I am so special?* I thought. The question had caught me off guard. I should have known. I should have been better prepared. I was beginning to have some inklings about how my mother's mind worked, and her comments didn't make me feel very safe as I continued to rummage through the refrigerator for food. I should have known my triumph was too bright and too public. *Damn! I should have kept my big mouth shut and gloated in private! I should never have told them I was even in a play.*

She had landed a direct hit. God love her, she was a pro at bursting bubbles. She knew my soft spots. She had me on the ground and wasn't about to let up. I withdrew my head from the refrigerator and carefully turned to face the jury that waited behind me.

"You're not so special, and don't think for a minute that you are. Don't you go and start getting all full of yourself." She was moving in for the kill. I was silent, bewildered, but still holding on.

"Well, I did a really good job, didn't I? That was a hard role to do," I said, stumbling to find my balance and answering without much backbone or resolve. I was on shaky ground. I wasn't sure how to fight her. A part of me always believed that what my mother told me must be heeded. There must be some life-saving gem of wisdom in all she said.

"Well, you did a *fine* job, just don't let it go to your head," was her final judgment—case closed.

I clung to the word fine like it was T-bone steak on a table of Ritz crackers. "Well, fine then. Fine is fine," I stammered. "I'm pretty tired. I'm going to bed now," and I turned to carry my plate stacked high with cheese, summer sausage, and crackers up to my room where I would reflect on the recent events.

As I sat at my desk eating my impromptu meal and listening to *Pet Sounds*, I wasn't sure what to make of the commotion that filled my head. I knew I had done a great job. I felt I didn't deserve to feel bad about doing a great job. I mean, *shouldn't* you feel good after you've done something really well? It was all a blur, a perplexing moment, when the emerging teen self gets caught in the crossfire of parental training. Wanting to shine like the sun while still living at home in the fog.

It was dawning on me that my mother might just be a bit off base in some of her lifestyle observations. She might be one of those glass-half-empty people, while I was a glorious and resplendent glass-half-full person Besides, she couldn't recognize real talent if it bit her in the ass. My ego was wounded. My feelings were hurt. She would not take away what I had done. I would not let her make me believe that my performance was mediocre.

I let Brian Wilson's maudlin ode to teenage angst wash over my wound, my cheese, sausage, and crackers:

I keep looking for a place to fit in where I can speak my mind,

I've been trying hard to find people that I won't leave behind,

They say I got brains, but they ain't doing me no good,
I wish they could.

Every time I get the inspiration to go change things around,

No one wants to help me look for places where these things might be found,
Where can I go when my fair weather friends cop out? What's it all about?

I wasn't mediocre. I was brilliant. I just had to make sure nobody else knew it.

. . .

That June I'd drawn the short straw among my three brothers in determining who would work for my father over the summer. He had four workhorses and only needed three. So it was up to me to find employment elsewhere. A friend of mine suggested I apply for a job at the John Michael Kohler Arts Center in downtown Sheboygan where they were looking for a part-time janitor. Since I was well versed in shoveling shit and working like an ox, it didn't take Frank Stolzenburger, the Director of Custodial Services, long to decide that I was the right guy for his minimum-wage job.

For a minker, it was ridiculously easy work to be paid for. I cleaned bathrooms, cut the lawn, and took orders from Frank. When Frank wasn't around to yell at me for not scrubbing the bathrooms clean enough, I would loiter in the art classes or sit in the back of the 350-seat theater watching rehearsals. There was something about these Art People that was nothing at all like my practical German ancestors. They were colorful birds—a flock of flakes and dreamers who called to me. They seemed to be inviting me to join them. *Come, Chucky. Leave the mink farm, the manure, and flies behind and come play with us. Do nothing but play and play and play,* I could hear the voice inside my head whisper. This was a decidedly different voice than the one that called to me from the church tabernacle. It was a more muffled voice, like it had a gag over its mouth and was being held hostage in the trunk of some car. At first it was hard for me to heed this siren call. My psyche had been carefully sculpted to keep its head down, work hard, tell the truth, and praise the Lord. But slowly over the course of that summer, I began to realize the world was divided between people who dream and play and those who work and go to church.

This growing fascination prompted me to return to the art center in the evenings and volunteer to work backstage painting sets and mingling with the actors and actresses. I was getting art wired and discovered yet another reason to love Art People—they had Art Women. I found the colorful personalities and expressive sensuality of these women alluring. But none rang my bell louder than the tasty, creative, and diminutive Stephanie Richter.

I met Stephanie one night while painting sets for a play her parents were starring in. Her parents, Norm and Mary Richter, were the Paul Newman and JoAnn Woodward of Sheboygan. They had their pick of the choicest roles. It got a little tiring seeing them strut their stuff in just about every play produced in town. Norm was especially painful to watch. He was short and barrel-chested with a big voice. Though he was five feet five inches tall, he played all his characters as if they were six feet. The local theatergoers loved him. They gloried in his schmaltzy, melodramatic performances. He was another in a long line of frustrated actors, toiling by day as the Director of Quality Control for the Wig-Wam Sock Company and performing at night in any show he could get cast in.

The Richters were the family I should have been born into. A family of artists and art lovers, a family that lived on the edge of a small, magical pond outside of Sheboygan. Their home was filled with books, cut flowers, old Persian rugs, and funky furniture. They even had solar reflectors to make hot water! Just the thought of creative humans co-habitating under one roof sent my heart pounding, but the knowledge that the perfect, beautiful, and exotic Stephanie lived there as well made this home on a magical pond appear to be paradise.

Unlike Molly Murphy, who was out of my league, Stephanie was within the range of my moderately magnetic personality. She had the face of an angel and the body of a yoga instructor. As we painted set pieces and carried costumes backstage, we talked in the language of expectant love—more my expectant love than hers, but who cares? She was, after all, my idealized version of art and love. To her I would direct the inner workings of my heart. With her, I would share my unrealized dreams and passions.

She had just graduated from high school and would be enrolled at Juilliard that fall, where she would study the dramatic arts and modern dance. I envied her but didn't have a clue why. I didn't realize what burned within me was the beating heart of an artist. While I was trying to figure out what I really wanted to do with my life, she was about to sail off to popular acclaim on the great stages of the world. Her parents had painted her wings in glorious rainbow colors, while mine were being repeatedly and decisively clipped.

She wore cotton tie-dyed clothing, white peasant dresses, and blouses embroidered in scenes from south of the border—little men with sombreros, sad-looking donkeys, gothic churches, and colorful plants and flowers. And to top it all off, her parents thought I was interesting and—potentially—talented.

One evening after a blissful session of painting stage scenery, I invited Stephanie to come out to my house. I knew my parents would be gone to a church function and the coast would be clear for a few hours of casual necking and groping. After a few more episodes like the one following my triumph in *The Lesson*, I became more guarded about which experiences and people I shared with my mother and which ones I needed to hide. Stephanie definitely fell into the second category.

As I pulled my father's pickup truck into the driveway, I was surprised to see my mother watering the flowers that grew around our home, but it was too late for me to turn and run. My mother was already pulling me in with her tractor beam. Putting the truck in reverse was out of the question. I had no choice but to face the music and introduce Stephanie to my mother. "Hi, Mom. This is Stephanie Richter. She, ah, paints scenery with me at the art center."

"Well, hello, Stephanie. How are you? You must be Norm and Mary's daughter," my mother said.

"I'm just fine, Mrs. Ries, it's so nice to meet you. You have a beautiful home and what lovely flowers," Stephanie, who was the epitome of good manners and cheerful demeanor, responded. God, she was smooth. I became hopeful that she could melt through my mother's armored defenses.

While Stephanie went into the house to use the bathroom, I was left alone with my mother, who lost no time in continuing her lifelong effort to refine my expectations. "Don't think you're going to marry a pretty girl."

"What do you mean, *marry*?" I replied. "We're just hanging out together."

"You know what I mean. Just don't think you're going to marry a pretty girl."

"She's going to Juilliard to study dance and acting. Isn't that great, Mom? She's a very nice girl."

"Not everyone needs to go to college, you know. You can stay right here in Sheboygan. Become an electrician or something. You can marry a nice local girl and do your acting at night," she said. As I stood in a pool of misery outside the back door of our home, I wondered if my mother was out of her mind. Besides, Stephanie was a local girl. But definitely not the type of *local* my mother had in mind for me.

This would not be the last time my mother would intercede to save me from setting my expectations too high. In great and small ways, she would continue to refine my dreams and my self-image. She was just doing her job—passing along to me the tools that she had learned and lived by. She grew up in a poor family and lived through the Great Depression. She didn't have many choices about what work she would do or what she would become. She was tough, steady, and not easily thrown by life's ups and downs. She never complained. If she was unhappy, she kept it to herself.

My mother's parents emigrated from Lithuania in 1904. They had four children. After high school she took a job as a house servant with a prominent local family. Had my grandfather Frank not loved to drink so much, my mother might not have had to start her career at such a young age, but she didn't complain. She never did.

I never knew whether to consider my Grandpa Franky an alcoholic or not. Among my hometown's Eastern European and German descendants, drinking was a bit like breathing air, and my grandfather could take in a great deal of air in one sitting. He had a habit of disappearing into a bar on payday and taking root until closing. My mother would tell stories of my grandmother's vigilance in making sure she headed him off at the pass, grabbing his paycheck before he liquefied it.

Despite a grinding, low-paying job delivering coal, he loved life, laughed, and was happy with his lot. I'd sit on his knee while he listened to the Milwaukee Braves on the radio. He'd hold a fly swatter in one hand and a bottle of Kingsbury beer in the other. He'd happily share a few sips of his beer with me until I fell asleep in his lap. He had survived a hard life and he drank to it with gusto. If he was a drunk, he was a very happy one. But my grandmother didn't necessarily share his happiness. It was she who counted the pennies and struggled to make ends meet. They had many long and loud fights over money, drinking, and work. Like many children of alcoholics, my mother learned to please and compromise, silently resolving never to have such a life for herself. She'd keep her expectations low—work hard and stay focused. She wouldn't fight. And while she may have had disagreements with my father, she kept them all inside for the sake of peace and harmony.

This mental toughness was never more evident than the day my mother moved to a nursing home and joined my father, who had gone there the year before. While this would be the last day she would spend in the home she had built with my father, lived in for fifty-six years, and raised seven children in, she made no more about leaving it than she would if she were going to the grocery store. It was just part of life. When the final moment came, she began walking out the door and then stopped. I thought she was going to have an emotional moment, one last soulful good-bye to her home of fifty-six years. Instead, she reached into her purse, took out her house key and said, "I won't need this anymore." She put the key on the kitchen table and went out the door without another word. She never looked back. She wasn't the sort of woman to look back. I have gotten more choked up about leaving apartments I lived in for a year than my mother did about leaving a home she had spent most of her life in.

As her final days neared, she complained that Jesus was taking too long in coming to get her. "Well, then, just tell Jesus He'd better hurry up," Joe told her.

"I have! I made it clear to Him I wasn't happy about waiting around. I told Him I was one of His best customers and I didn't understand what was taking so long. Sometimes I just can't figure that guy out!" That was my mom—God loving, God fearing, and Godawfully faithful. But, goddamn it, God better come through with His end of the bargain. She'd done her duty, kept to the Good Book, and been faithful to her less-than-fun husband for fifty-six years, and now she wanted Him to pick her up in a chariot of angels and return her home— and she wanted it done yesterday!

While my mother suffered a few physical ailments in her twilight years, she was generally in good health. It was only after my father passed away that she declared she was ready to go and began to fade away. A few weeks before she died and just eleven months after my father's passing, she visited Joe's home. At this point my mother had lost all interest in eating. But Joe persisted in encouraging her to eat or drink something—a soda, hot cocoa, or hot soup. Unpredictably, she said, "give me a Brandy Old Fashion. I guess I'm old enough to have an Old Fashion anytime I want." She was eighty-six.

As the weeks went by, she grew weaker, and we knew the time was near. Each of us said our final good-byes and told her why we loved her. We thanked her for giving us those rules to live by and preparing us for life. For making us the sort of people who could deal with life's sorrows and bounce back, people who tried to do the right thing and showed up every day to play whatever cards we were given. We told her that we loved her.

A few hours before her death, the nurse called to tell us our mother was dying and we'd better hurry or we would miss her passing. Four of my siblings were in her room as she began to fade and heard her ask my oldest sister, Kathleen, "Did I do the right thing with Sue's baby?" Sue's baby was her first grandchild, and it would be her life's final worry.

For thirty years my mother never talked about Sue's baby. Not since she came to my bedroom that night in September, woke me from a deep sleep, and said, "Your sister's going to have a baby out of wedlock. We're going to put it up for adoption." That was it. She didn't wait for questions. She had done her job and took her pain and disappointment and placed it deep within her heart until moments before she would die.

"Yes, Mom, you did the right thing. You can go now. Sue's baby is fine. We're all fine. You've taken care of us all. It's okay to go," Kathleen replied as she held my mother's hand.

"Are you sure?"

"Positive, Mom. You can go now."

With the permission my sister had given her, my mother's eyes wandered to the ceiling and a slight smile broke over her lips as if she was seeing something or someone. With her last breath, she said, "Good, it was the right thing to do." Her worries were over. Her work was done. All of her children were accounted for. She was, at that moment, free to return home.

17.

Birdman

"RIES, I'm running for class president. This place needs a change of attitude. I couldn't stand having another one of those Brooks Brothers pinheads lead us again, or worse, a triple letterman. I'll puke. I swear, I'll puke right here. Will someone please get me out of this place? I should have left high school three years ago. I should have just skipped it. My youth has been squandered. But as long as we're here, let's have some fun. Let's confuse the sleeping masses and shake things up. I'm running for class president and I want you to be my campaign manager," Andy Wertzelski said as we stood outside of the gym. He was someone from my generation who was doing what Bob and his friends talked about.

Someone was bound to slip over the stockade that surrounded Sheboygan and bring with him the seeds of social discontent and the counterculture.

Olive skinned, dark haired, and medium height, Andy looked like a handsome Italian, but he was actually of Slovenian descent. His mouth poured out a torrent of new thoughts and his hands danced alongside them. A year ahead of me in school, he wore a respectable mustache and longish hair that marked him as a budding student radical. Just as Marco Polo brought silk and spices from the Far East in the fourteenth century, Andy brought the new, the wild, and the progressive into the safe harbor of our high school. And as with most prophets, the sleeping, beer-drinking masses ignored him.

To us it wasn't just a campaign for president of our student body; it was a metaphor for the radical changes we felt were needed. It was an opportunity to get our message out there and, if Andy were to win, a chance to let the rhetoric fly at graduation. He would stand before five hundred graduating seniors and their parents in June and let them hear the unadorned truth about the war, freedom of speech, and life—all from the unique perspective of Andrew Wertzelski. There would be no candy-coating the truth. Didn't someone once say "The truth will set you free"? Well, we would not only win the election, we would open the closed and apathetic minds of our classmates. We'd revolutionize our school and our community, and at the head of the parade would be Andy—Truth-teller, harbinger of a new era of enlightenment. *All hail Andy! Wertzelski for President! People, cast off your television sets and come join the glorious revolution!*

We chose a minimalist approach for our campaign and grabbed the popular image of Che Guevara, the dead Central American revolutionary hero whose picture had become an icon of the counterculture—full beard, black beret, steely black eyes, chiseled good looks, and the expression of a man on a mission. Along with the stenciled image of Che, we added the message WERTZELSKI FOR RADICAL CHANGE! Andy's opponent was my Young Republican cousin, Steve Ries, and this allowed us to create a second short campaign slogan—BETTER RED THAN RIES! The ideological lines were drawn—vote for freedom or vote for a guy who starched his underwear.

But we realized that the medium was also the message. A simple wall poster and clever nomination speech would not be enough to worm our way into the petrified minds of our classmates. So we decided that Andy had to *become* Che. Fortunately for the Andrew Wertzelski

Campaign Committee, we had a candidate who actually looked a great deal like Che himself. Our crack team of image consultants had Andy grow a beard and begin to wear a beret with the distinctive red star embroidered on the front. When he walked down the hall, people stopped and took notice. He looked impressive. A few Neanderthals tossed ridicule his way, but Andy took it all in stride. Prophets had always been taunted and persecuted by the ruling elite. It came with the job— revolution was hard work. It didn't matter that the electorate didn't know there was a Cultural Revolution taking place. It didn't matter that they listened to *1910 Fruitgum Company* and *The Allman Joys* while we listened to *Jethro Tull, Jimi Hendrix*, and *Country Joe McDonald*. No, none of this mattered because we knew Andrew Wertzelski would soon be our leader. We plastered the hallways with his Che-ized likeness; we handed out pins with the image of Che on them; and offered our classmates bubblegum and donuts at the front door of the school. We painted Andy's car with our campaign slogan and the symbol of our struggle. We played political hardball and tried to show my right-wing cousin that lefties could appeal to the same base instincts of the slumbering masses that he did. If we could have bought them all a six-pack of Pabst Blue Ribbon beer, we would have. We were out to win. The left would be right.

When Andy saw the first stenciled posters come off the press, he shouted, "This is excellent, fucking excellent, Ries! God, we're brilliant. This will stir the souls of those pudding heads. It will release a deep, archetypal longing for radical change. We will free them from their shackles. We'll wake them up to the war, and they'll join in our struggle against the corrupt self-interests of the political right. *I am Che. Che for President. Che. Che. Che!*" Andy began to hop and jump like an Indian on a warpath. He was happy. He was fomenting change. He was born for revolution.

Andy's run for office failed. We lost in a landslide to my cousin. We'd misjudged the willingness of the masses to be led by the nose into political reform. We needed more than donuts and bubblegum to win this election. We should have paid them money to vote for Andy. But we took our election loss in stride. It would only make us stronger.

Despite his defeat, Andy remained tireless. He continued to irritate teachers and search for the edge. He introduced me to Carlos Castaneda and his peyote-eating shaman, Don Juan. I had my first joint with him and he gave me the WORD. My generation didn't invent the word, but we spread it like pollen, raised it to art and anger, and embraced it as a true friend. We gave it a home in our mouths. Long before it landed on my generation, it wandered through both obscure and noteworthy literature. It showed up in 1922 in James Joyce's *Ulysses* and again in D. H. Lawrence's *Lady Chatterley's Lover.* But it wasn't until Lenny Bruce ate the word and gave it wings in the early sixties that it hit the big time. It jumped from the underworld to popular culture. And while other words have gone on to silent deaths, this one seemed only to gain momentum with use. It became noun, adjective, and adverb. It was spoken not just in the back streets, but also in high society. It remains to this day a timeless treasure that keeps on giving and continues to define any moment, from the sexual, to the mundane, to the glorious. If the bird was the word, then Andy Wertzelski was the birdman.

After graduation, Andy enrolled at the University of Wisconsin–Madison and found an environment every bit as wild and progressive as he was. When it came to the word, Andy roared down the freeway like a Maserati hell-bent for hot leather. He used it often and with such variety, speed, and abandon that he'd become its maestro.

He extracted the many hues, feelings, and nuances of the word. He was on fucking fire.

"Hey, Ries, how the fuck are you doing, buddy? Madison welcomes you. This place is un-fucking-believable. Welcome to America's parallel universe. Too bad you're still doing time in Sheboygan when all this good shit is going down here in wonderland. I mean the war will be over by the time you fucking get out of high school. Have a beer and a joint, brother. It'll ease your mind," Andy said, as he greeted me at the door to his dorm room. "It's the Miller High Life—dope, beer, women, and fuck the government; fuck the war. I'm fucking in love with this place! You're going to march tonight, aren't you? It's going to be absofuckinglutely huge. They don't have a clue what the rules are. Well, fuck them and fuck me and fuck us all!" he raged on in the uninterrupted, staccato fashion of a guy who had just consumed four hits of white cross and three beers, and was completing his second joint. Andy was on a roll, and I was becoming vaguely concerned that he might drive right over me in the process. The freight train handed me another beer.

"I'm going. I wouldn't miss it for anything. I'm ready to do my part to stop the war," I replied with relative enthusiasm.

"Stop the war? Start the fucking partying! Here, have another beer and a few hits off this. It's awesome stuff. It'll do you good," he said, passing me a can of beer and a joint.

The clashes between the police and student demonstrators had become hostile in Madison and on many other campuses throughout the country. The weekly marches, sit-ins, and rallies presented the perfect opportunity for young people to run wild for a good cause. I'd seen the news reports. The police had started to wear riot gear. They removed the windows of their vans and replaced them with chicken wire to prevent bottles and rocks from doing serious damage. They carried nightsticks and wore helmets and were ready to strap on gas masks when the first canisters of tear gas were fired into the crowd. Our opponents were big, porky guys who favored crew cuts. There was no confusing us with them. *God, this was great! No gray at all. Everything is black and white. How could life get any better than this? Stoned, drunk, and radicalized.*

"Yup, I'm absofuckinglutely going!" I said, trying one of Andy's variations of the word on for size.

The intoxicants had successfully lowered my sense of self-consciousness and high anxiety. I could feel myself entering the flow zone—a place of mindless, guilt-free adolescence. "You're fucking right I'm going!" I shouted, feeling my newfound freedom surging within me. "Whatever the fuck happens, I'm ready for it."

"That's fucking great, Ries. You da' fucking man. The pigs will be out in full force. It will be a fucking party!" Andy rambled on and on and on as all people high on speed do. They also believe they've just been awarded a temporary one hundred point IQ increase. They are now one of the cleverest, most courageous, and best-looking people in the room.

Library Mall is a small, open park that sits between Memorial Library and the State Historical Society. When Andy and I arrived, there were over 30,000 students assembled. Across the street we saw twenty police vans with hundreds of officers lined up in front of them—helmets on, facemasks down, and nightsticks in hand. If I'd been sober, I would have run back to the dorm room, but instead I marveled at the throng that spread before me. "Shit. Impressive. Look at this crowd!" I said, feeling that I was looking at a herd of buffalo as it stretched from horizon to horizon. A sight so immense and grand it couldn't be real.

"What a crowd!" Andy said as he raised his two arms high above his head, the palms of his hands facing forward as if he were blessing each and every person standing before him. "This is going to be excellent! Fucking believe it, Ries-ski. This is war and we're not going to fucking take it anymore. Here, have another beer," he said as he pulled a can from his backpack and handed it to me. "You gotta be fucked up to riot," he said, not needing to convince me.

"Okay, everybody, shut up and listen!" a bullhorn from the front steps of the library bellowed, "We have a job to do. Our government is breaking the law and we're going let them know we don't like it. We're going to march in the streets. We're going to stop the traffic. We'll shut this university and this town down! We're going to stop the war!!!"

A roar of approval rose from the crowd and the first round of chanting began, *Ho Ho Ho Chi Minh! The NLF is Gonna Win!* Sixty thousand feet stamped the dry surface of the mall. A brown dust cloud rose to envelop the throng as dusk turned to night. The herd was getting restless. A rhythmic pounding rose up over the crowd as an enthusiastic group pounded on the steel sheets that covered the mall water fountain for the winter. The stampede was about to begin.

"Okay, shut up and listen!" the march leader shouted again. "We're heading out in three groups," he said and cut the crowd into three slices using his arm as a knife. Each section was told which route to follow. "We'll meet up at the State Capitol in one hour. They'll use gas and clubs. We have to hang together. Pigs don't like being televised beating college students, so make damn sure you've got the cameras on you if you're getting pounded." The chanting began again. *One, two, three four; we don't want your fucking war!* As we headed out from the mall, the police wasted no time in shooting tear gas canisters into our midst. The more skilled and well-prepared brethren strapped on gas masks, put gloves on their hands, and started picking up smoking tear gas canisters and heaving them back at the cops. The race was on. Oh, the glory of running from the police for the cause of righteousness on a late autumn day in Wisconsin!

The three carefully drawn groups quickly disintegrated into chaos. It was every man and woman for himself or herself. We ran fast and hard. The reality of the experience had overloaded my circuits. I was scared and I wasn't too proud to fucking admit it. Blinded by the tear gas, people were being beaten and tossed into police vans. Tempers were running wild, and I wondered what I was doing out here. Instantly, I turned into a pacifist and sprinted back to Andy's dorm room.

After an hour, Andy showed up with a torn shirt, ripped jeans, and a large lump on his forehead, "Shit, the pigs almost nailed me. Well, I guess they did nail me. I feel like I got a fucking watermelon growing out of my head. The thing hurts like hell. Goddamned pigs. I was an inch away from being arrested. The pig had me by my shirt collar and then some drug-crazed son of a bitch jumps him from behind. What a fucking great time! Hey, you want a joint and a beer?" he asked, as if he'd just returned from grocery shopping.

"No, I think I'll just be sober for awhile."

"Suit yourself, Ries. But there's nothing like a riot to give the soldier of democracy one hell of a Pabst Blue Ribbon thirst," he said, sprawling on his bunk with an ice pack on his head and a cold beer in his hand.

While I loved the idea of revolution, I didn't have the stomach for knocking heads with the police. I was trying to escape the thumbprint of Riesville, but when all was said and done, I couldn't be as crazy as I wanted myself to be. Not all costumes are meant to be worn and not all prophets can be followed. I'd keep looking.

18.

The 360-Degree Pee

BY THE fall of my senior year I'd completed all the classes I needed to apply for college and decided to explore the electives that were offered. Growing more comfortable in my identity as a member of the counterculture, I signed up for a small engine class. Other than running track drills through the far west corridor, I never walked down this hall where classes for future piston heads and factory workers were held.

I walked into class on the first day and took my position at the table that would be my workstation for the next three months. It would be here that I'd learn the inner workings of the finicky one cylinder engine— commonly called "the lawnmower." Across from me was Michael Buss. I only knew Mike to say hello to. He didn't play sports. He kept to himself. I didn't share any other classes with him. He was one of the invisible people.

"Ries, what are *you* doing here? You lost? You don't need this shit to go to college," he said.

"I thought I'd learn a little about how the small engine built America. I can't tell a piston ring from a carburetor. I figure it's time to learn. Besides, I wanted to try something different. I'm tired of hanging around with honors students," I said, unaware that I sounded like an arrogant prick.

"If you want to try something different, why not take Home Ec? At least they got lots of chicks to help you make your brownie batter better," he said. We both laughed at the simple logic of his observation and, after he'd pointed this out me, I too wondered why I hadn't signed up for Baking 101.

Mike never made another mention of why I was there. He took me at my word and took me for who I was and we started fixing lawnmower engines.

We each took our engines apart while keeping a careful inventory of the parts and where they fit, and otherwise making sure we'd be able to put the damn thing back together again. I was a blaze of efficiency in dismantling my engine, but when it came to putting it together again, I began to sputter. "Ries, what kind of a mess you got there, buddy?" Mike asked, in his usual monotone manner.

"Ya, I'm having some problems getting these piston rings back. How'd you do that? I broke the last four," I said, raising my greased hands up in a sign of surrender.

"You've got problems a lot bigger than your piston rings, dumb shit. I don't want to stick my nose in your business, but you'll never get that thing started. It's a fucking mess. You've killed it," he deadpanned. "I've had my eye on you, Ries. Waiting for the moment you'd pull the ignition cord and it'd piss a pint of Pennzoil all over that button-down baby blue shirt of yours. You should stick to theater and politics, and let real men fix your engines," he said.

"To hell with real men, I need help getting this thing together. For Christ sakes, I'm going to flunk an engine class. You're right, I should have taken Home Ec." We laughed and Mike did what he could to bring life back to my engine. When class was over we went our separate ways until the following day when our worlds would meet again.

. . .

The lunch hour was over and I'd stopped in the john

to take a leak when a hardhead from the west corridor, Steve Dunbar, walked in with two of his pet apes, Jim Heinz and Mike Madison. The threesome smelled like cigarettes, beer, and car grease. They were incapable of being any place quietly. They walked loud, talked loud, punching each other, the bathroom door, or anything else within reach of their fists. It didn't matter the place or time of day, it was always time to hit something.

I was preparing to do my business as they entered the men's bathroom when Dunbar came up behind me and slugged me in a little too friendly manner on the shoulder, "Hey, scrambled eggs for brains. This isn't your fucking pee-can. It's time for you to go."

At that moment, Buss walked in and while not seeing the initial blow, made a quick assessment, deciding that Dunbar wasn't standing behind me to give me a shoulder rub and said, "Fuck you, Dunbar."

"Fuck you. Fuck me. Fuck him," Dunbar replied, turning and pounding my shoulder a second time.

Realizing that drastic action was required, I began to urinate and turned a 360-degree circle applying a well-placed bead of pee across the kneecaps of Dunbar and his two henchmen. Having completed my triple axle-spinning leap, I returned to my frontal pissing position and finished my business and Buss was beaming. He was in awe. He didn't say a word as I zipped up my fly and turned to face Dunbar who was groping for the word, but could only produce a non-syllabic gasp of air.

"Oh...ffff...dam...my pants. You fucking peed on my pants! Are you nuts?! You fucking peed on my pants. You little fucking balls for brains, you queer little homo fucked-up little shit. I'll kill you. My pants. You peed on my pants!"

I wasn't clever enough to come up with such a disarming tactic as innovative as the 360-Degree Pee. I give full credit to Tom Wilson, one of my fellow Black Birds, who, one night after an eighth grade basketball game, demonstrated it to nine teammates who were unfortunate enough to be standing behind him. But it was only then, three years later, with a prick breathing fire down my neck, that his brilliant move came back to me. I power-peed to save my life.

"You lay a hand on my friend and I will shove your head up your ass, Dunbar. We might never find you again, you got such a fucking big ass," Buss said. While Mike was a solid guy, he was no match for Dunbar. What made him scary was that he didn't care if he lost. A much-talked-about fistfight the year before left him on the ground and beaten, but he never shed a tear and never asked for mercy. Buss was one of those mild-mannered guys who went ape shit when they lost their temper. He transcended and became a swinging pain-free zone. You might win, but you would suffer and you would not get the pleasure of his asking for mercy.

The moment of reflective silence laid at the feet of these two mountain rams. Dunbar did not want to butt heads with Buss and motioned his two apes to the door snorting one final, "Fuck you, Buss, good thing that putz has you to do his fighting for him," and he left.

Mike raised his eyebrows and said, "Woo, I'm scared. In fact, I'm so scared I think I'll take a ten-foot piss," and proceeded to unzip, take aim, and hit the urinal with an arc of triumph. We were both laughing as we left the boys' room, giving high fives and saying we'd see each other in small engines class tomorrow.

I didn't get into fights, so "protection" was pretty much wasted on me, but once the word got out that messing with Ries meant you messed with Buss, a fight never came close to me. I didn't see Mike much after our class was over and when we saw each other in the hall, he was as silent and polite as ever, just a nod of the head and a, "How's it going Ries? Make any good brownies lately?"

19.

Love Lost

I WAS good at the quick hit, the brilliant first impression and snappy connection that didn't require sustained focus, so when it came to the migratory desire of all adolescents to find romantic love and an endearing relationship, I was ill equipped. My parents weren't into public displays of affection. I never saw them hug or kiss one another. I never had any of the now popular heart-to-heart talks about life with them. The ones where the modern dad or the modern mom asks, "How are you feeling?" Feelings were an alien species in our home—a devalued asset in a world where getting things done and doing the right thing were first and foremost. Feelings happen when one is allowed to rest and vacation, when one stops all *doing* and allows what's floating around inside to bubble up and introduce itself. Our family never took vacations and we never stopped doing. We weren't bubbly people.

But being bad at romance never stopped me from trying to have it. Lacking any mentoring or role modeling in this aspect of life, I did what millions of left-footed dancers do every day: I tried to dance. I had a few short, confused stints with girlfriends. I wanted to be vaporized, saved, and remade in the wonder of the feminine mystique—a process I rather simplistically thought of as *sex*. To me sex *was* romance or, at least, it was the active ingredient in romance that I instinctively related to.

I was born hornier than most. It was my special gift. A *blessing*, if used it to honor and serve the Lord. Or a *curse*, if used for evil. Unfortunately there were no athletic letters I could earn for being horny. No championship rings I could win in order to get my picture on the front page of the school newspaper proclaiming *Ries Wins State Sex Marathon—Sets New Record for Height and Distance*. Alas, God had given me a gift that was both wonderful and complicated. So much so I thought the devil had set up camp in my crotch.

A civil war raged within me—one side wanted affirmation, romance, and the healing waters of a woman—while the other side just wanted sex. I walked this tight-rope without guide or safety net. I fumbled my way as best I could. I'd invite shapely smart girls to help me with my math or science in the hope we'd do *something* after the homework was over. *Something* was whatever I could lay my hands on. There was no plan other than this prime directive to find release, and it didn't take much. A few moments rolling on the floor entangled with my math tutor would quickly result in the tell-tale sign of sexual climax soaking though the front of my bell bottom jeans and—with it—guilt, silence and sadness. "Chuck, you okay? Did I do something wrong? You seem awfully quiet all of sudden." My lovely math tutor would say.

"No. I'm fine. I mean, you're fine. I just remembered a sad story I read earlier today about a crippled, quadriplegic widow with six kids and no hope for the future. I can't seem to get it out of my head. Why does God allow such injustices to exist?" I lied.

"It's a shame," my tutor noted, "but that's a pretty weird thing to be thinking about at a time like this. Don't you think?"

It was a lie—a white lie. I'd blown my load and I was mentally working my way through eighteen years of programming that told me what I'd just done was a sin and, by default, I was a mean, nasty, disgusting person. This was the great paradox of my sexual yearning; its fulfillment only worsened its curse.

. . .

Gloria Cavallari had just gotten her teaching degree from a small Christian college in Ohio—the kind of place parents sent their children to protect them from the counterculture's attack on family values. She was a full-figured woman of Italian descent, with a ready smile, long brunette hair, and large brown eyes. She loved life and brought with her the unbridled enthusiasm of a first-year teacher. Wearing the trademark floral dress, sandals, and loopy earrings of the late sixties, she'd just turned twenty-one years old and been given one of East High's two prized Honors Humanities classes to teach.

"Who's heard of Hermann Hesse's *Siddhartha*?" she asked us. When no one answered, she continued, "Well, that's good, because you're all going to love this story. It's about finding yourself. Hermann Hesse is a wonderful author. We're all going on a journey this year to discover who we are and who we want to be. Great literature helps each of us find our way. It brings us different voices to try on for size. We'll love some authors and others we won't relate to, but all of them will swirl around in our head. And that's what I want to accomplish this year. I want to make your heads ache with ideas," she laughed, pleased to be passing along the things she loved.

We were a bright group and she gave us everything in her bookcase: S. R. Suzuki's *East West*, Jean Paul Sartre's *No Exit*, Albert Camus' *The Stranger*, Ralph Ellison's *Invisible Man*, Dostoyevsky's *Brothers Karamazov* and Carl Jung's *Dreams, Memories, and Reflections*. If we wanted more, she gave us new titles and authors to read. I read all of Hermann Hesse in a month and then plowed through the great humanist, Albert Camus. When I was finished with that I began to read through the existential philosophy of Sartre. Here were authors who spent their lives considering the meaning of life. I was finding that I was not the only tortured soul who'd ever lived. I took refuge in these authors and became a sponge for the mystic, the political, and the esoteric.

Gloria Cavallari was an only child. She didn't have the luxury of getting lost in a big family crowd or having siblings bring new ideas to the dinner table. While my escape was in endlessly doing, hers was in reading. We both yearned for meaning. When I fell in love with an idea

I didn't modulate my passion for it as she did. I jumped headfirst into it. She walked and smiled. I sprinted and grimaced. She was an island of sweetness and insight. We were twins born to different families.

Gloria was also one of the yearbook advisors and, since I wrote articles on the selective service and the draft for the school newspaper, it was only natural that I'd find my way to working on the yearbook. We were soon spending two to three hours a day together. She had a small loyal entourage of followers who adored her, a flock of kindred spirits who could be found sitting around her desk after school or between classes talking about life, literature, and popular culture.

"You've met *da'Wert*, haven't you—Andy Wertzelski? Brilliant, but a real nut case. I joined him for the march in Madison last week. Things got out of hand. I'm not sure I want to do that again. Just what I need—to get arrested and bailed out of jail by my parents," I told her as I worked on the layout for the yearbook.

"You should be careful. They're not putting up with much anymore. A lot of students were arrested and hurt. So what do you think you're going to do about the draft? They aren't granting anymore college deferments."

"I'm working on filing for conscientious-objector

status. If I don't get it, I'm not sure what I'll do. Go to Canada most likely."

"It's sad. All those lives being lost. I feel totally helpless to do anything about it except pray," she said and became quiet for a moment.

"Well, you might march. Send a few letters to your elected official or something," I said.

"It's not my thing. I'd rather stay close to home and do what good I can, one person at a time. I don't think God created me to change the world. Maybe change a few lives along the way, but not the world. That's for high velocity people like you. Overflowing with too much juice to sit still. Hey, I'm having some kids over for dinner tomorrow night. You want to come? I think you know Randy and Brenda Koerpers, don't you? Clara Weidemeyer is coming too."

"Yup, I know the Koerpers. And Clara, well, she's done more with less than anyone I know. I'm sure the Koerpers will want to read tarot cards and summon the spirits. It's their favorite pastime. They're always doing one thing or another with the occult. How about you? You too Catholic to commune with the spirits of our dead ancestors?"

"I'm open to trying anything as long as it doesn't hurt

anyone. We'll just make sure we conjure up good fun spirits. How about that?"

"It's a deal."

. . .

Over the next three months, we became friends. I thought that at some point she'd tire of me and start hanging out with people her own age, this despite that only three years separated us.

It was an early winter afternoon and we'd just returned to her small second floor walkup after a long walk along the lakefront. Sitting with our feet a few inches from the space heater, we gazed into the heater's red coils as if they were logs on a fire. "You want a beer or some tea?" I asked.

"Beer for me," she said. The drinking age in Wisconsin was eighteen and sharing a beer was as common as going for a walk. Well, actually, sharing a beer was more common than going for a walk.

After I'd gotten the beer from the refrigerator, I turned to the poster she'd hung behind her stove with a picture of Florence, Italy, on it and meditated for a moment before saying, "Gloria, if I didn't know better, I'd say I was falling in love with you. But what do I know? Love,

love, love and lumps on my head, if I didn't know better, I'd be better off dead."

"Oh, stop it. There's nothing wrong with you or with love. Sort of the natural human condition to want it and want to give it away. Don't you think?" she said from the other room.

"Well, I guess I do. It's the virtuous cycle the Buddhists talk about. Selfless acts of love, creating happiness, which in turn creates more joy. Well, I think you're a lovely person. You've rescued me and you deserve an award. Too bad you're my goddamn high school teacher and not just some girl I met at the VFW. We could polka the night away and then double-dip ourselves in fish batter when we got home," I said, as I walked into the small living room and sat down next to her.

"You're my reward. You're the guy who tries hard to do the right things. Not easy getting over our past. Not easy to know what we're feeling beneath all the things we've been taught we should feel. But I don't think we have much choice in these things. They just come along and eat us alive. Sometimes I can hear it as clearly as you talking to me, or it might come in a dream—the *call*. It's so clear and so loud you just know it's the real thing— the right thing. Not psychological static, or fear—it's God helping us out, pointing us in a direction. It doesn't come too often, but when it does it directs us to exactly the place or the person or the work we need to find. You can run from it, but sooner or later you pay the price. You pay with your happiness. Trust the spirit in you, no matter what. That's what this wise old woman thinks."

"Hey, wake up! Remember me? I'm clueless about all things having to do with feelings, romance, and, most importantly, women."

"I don't believe you. I think you know exactly what you want and what you're feeling, but you don't trust it. You're not used to feeling. God's moving you toward your heart's desire. And you know what? It's going to feel weird; it might even hurt. So what. Do it anyway."

I had begun to forget that Gloria was an *adult*. It didn't seem that way. After four months of long conversations and sweet silences, the teacher had evaporated and a friend had taken her place—a friend who was helping me to hear a new voice in me. Only unlike the one I'd heard years ago being broadcast from the tabernacle, this one sounded benevolent. It wasn't censoring. It was inviting. Gloria and the world she was giving me were making me realize the things I yearned for weren't wrong just because they were ambitious, sexual, or intellectually provocative.

"Well, my dear, while you're drilling holes in your

psyche, why don't you open this gift I got for you," she said, pulling a wrapped present from under the sofa.

"I don't deserve it," I said, in the hoarse whisper of a man on his deathbed. "Can't you see I am not a man? I am a monster!" I continued in my best imitation of Lon Chaney in *The Hunchback of Notre Dame*. We broke out laughing at my pained confession.

"You play despicable very well. I see you've been busy torturing yourself again."

"You haven't seen anything yet," I said as I opened the gift she had got me. It was Joseph Campbell's *The Symbolic Quest*. "Looks like kind of a big book. Think I can handle it?"

"If you can handle Sartre and Nietzsche, this ought be like floating on air. You might find some things in here you've been looking for. Remember, you're not the only blind, deaf, and dumb person seeking the meaning of life."

I gave her a kiss on the cheek. We looked at each other for a long moment like two old friends who hadn't seen one another for many years. It was a bittersweet reunion as we realized how lonely life had been without the other. "Chuck, you're not the worst person God ever made, you know? They lied to you; your treasure room isn't empty—it's full. Now you have to start believing it.

Besides, you have at least three very redeeming qualities: you're cute, you worry too much about everything, and you have a great mind."

"Did I ever tell you the story about the first humans?" I asked her.

"You mean, humans like other humans or humans like us?"

"Like us," I replied. "The Greeks believed that before we walked alone as we do now, we were born complete. We were attached, back to back, to our perfect mate. We'd cartwheel through life with joy. Our joy was so utterly complete it made the gods jealous of us and, in a fit of anger, they cut all of us in two, sending our perfect halves to wander the earth in search of its loved one. They say that finding this soul mate may take many lifetimes. But when it happens, you know it. It's like that voice you were talking about—you just know," I said as my heart raced with the excitement of completion.

We'd grown close in slow, steady, silent inches. It happened despite our ignoring it. It happened, because it was meant to happen. We were disappearing and falling into each other.

The lid came off the butterfly jar that night and we raced to fill every available minute with each other. We never *officially* went to bed, nor did we have intercourse. But God had given us two hands and we let our ten fingers do the walking. We let them travel up and down the length and width of our two young bodies. And after one such extended pilgrimage, Gloria said, "Ever have a girl go down on you?"

"You mean a blowjob?"

"Yes, that's one vulgar term for it."

"I think that inner voice you've been telling me about is saying to proceed full speed ahead."

"Well, sounds like your inner voice is no dummy," and she proceeded to work her magic.

My God-given blessing was about to meet its match. While I wouldn't be winning either an athletic letter or a championship ring, I would have my bell rung. I focused the collective power of my mind and blocked out the voice that suddenly returned straight out of the tabernacle. The one sounding quite a bit like Charlton Heston doing his best imitation of Moses as a conservative Christian at a National Republican Convention, *Chuck, I just stopped by to warn you about this job you are getting. It may feel good, but it's a sin. It's a big whopper. Blowjobs are not some clever Catholic birth control device. Whoever put that idea into your head was not a friend of Mine. This is a no-no. You think masturbation was hard to get over, well, wait until you open this door. Wait until you've been blown. You shall forever wander the earth in search of more blowjobs. Your soul will have a thirst that cannot be quenched. You will be no better than a sick, depraved sex addict. Save thyself and flee. Flee from this woman who now labors over your loin.*

I struggled to turn the radio dial toward the new soul station in my mind. The one whose signal had been intermittently becoming more distinct until I heard the deep silky strains of the Minister of Love whispering, *Everything is cool, babe. Let that sweet, sweet love wash over you, babe. That's right, little mighty minkster, you just drop into the soulful river of romance. You got the Minister's imprimatur to praise the Lord through His gift of love. So you just drown in that sexy sea of pleasure and float away.* As Gloria put wind in my sail, I took a moment to praise the Minister and then submitted without resistance to the bouquet of lips my Italian princess was showering upon me.

"Look, just relax, close your eyes, and empty that over-active brain of yours. In fact, if there are any voices banging around in there, turn them all off right this minute and let me do the talking."

Resistance was futile—naked before the rose-colored glow of the space heater, I did as she commanded. And when she was done, my mind was a cosmic expanse of radio silence.

. . .

Throughout high school, I drove my dad's three-quarter ton, gold Chevy pickup truck. It wasn't too hard to spot. During the height of my heat with Gloria, I'd park it a few blocks away from her apartment when I visited. Despite this precaution, we'd had a few near misses when one classmate or another stopped by unannounced. Usually, we'd let them in, but this proved problematic one evening.

Gloria had lit the candles and incense. When the doorbell rang, we were way past undressing. Our erotic flames froze. We hoped that whoever was at the door would go away. *What would the Minister of Love do at a time like this?* I thought as my hard-on melted and Gloria and I stayed still, thinking motionlessness would make us invisible to the pair of eyes now peeping through the curtain that hung over the back-door window. We were well out of sight and, after a few minutes, the visitor left. But they could not have missed the fact that the candles were lit, yet no one was home.

By morning I was sure the headlines in the local press would proclaim the magnitude of our indiscretion. Worse, Gloria would lose her job and I would have placed an enormous X on the reputation of my parents, my ancestors, and every Ries who'd ever lived. I would single-handedly have destroyed my family's good name. The anxiety was crushing. I was so weak from fear that I feigned sickness the next day. My mother was surprised, as I never got sick, or, rather, we were never allowed to be sick. So I told her I couldn't walk, "Mom, I can't walk. I feel all clammy and dizzy. It's so odd, I just feel like I'm about to pass out or something," I grimaced, crossed my eyes, and willed myself into a fever as my mother put her hand to my forehead.

"Are you really sick? You don't feel hot. Your color is good," she replied, curious, but satisfied that if I felt I had to miss school, then indeed I should miss school.

I found out that it was Clara Weidemeyer who had stopped by the night before.

"Chuck, got a minute?" Clara asked as we were leaving school a few days later.

"Sure. What's up?" I said.

"I saw your truck a few blocks away from Gloria's the other night. I don't think anyone else noticed it. You don't have to come clean with me, but I think you'd better start being a little careful or this could be bad for you and her. You're both good people. I don't want things getting messed up for either of you."

"Nothing's happening. We're just good friends."

"I don't care if you're sleeping with her, but you'd better watch it. Vogel is thinking something is up. She can smell indiscretions a mile away. She's God's avenger. Created to bust all sinners. She has her eye on you two. If she can prove anything, you'll be in deep shit and Gloria could get fired," Clara finished. Over the four years since I became Clara's designated king, we'd become philosophical friends. We sat in the same honors classes and held the same views about the war and life in general. She was still the ugliest girl I'd ever met, but I'd become fond of her for her remarkable tenacity and rich insights.

"We're not so different, you know," Clara said. "We both want *something*. I'm not sure what it is either. I feel as restless as you do. I can see how the two of you click. It's a good thing. I wish I could find someone, but with this mug, my chances are pretty slim." Clara stopped for a moment as a classmate walked by, "This isn't smart, Chuck. No one will get it. They'll make a good thing bad. That's what they always do. So, I suggest you let it go."

We sat for a while longer on the cement planter outside

school as the buses and cars took our classmates home. I no longer cared who saw me talking to East's biggest dog. I was proud to be Clara's friend. She never asked one thing of me, other than to be true to myself. My dalliance with Gloria never leaked out.

. . .

Connie Vogel was Chairman of the Humanities Department. She was a first-class hardass and, while it was common knowledge that she was having an affair with Paul Fulker, the chemistry teacher, her midnight encounters were viewed as acts of mercy by the faculty. Since Fulker's wife had been terminally ill with cancer for many years, they figured he needed some tender loving care. Yet Vogel saw no inconsistency in trying to hunt down the rumor that Gloria and I were romantically involved.

"Gloria, I'm afraid the word might get out about us. I don't think it has. That was Clara who stopped by the other night. She's got a nose for trouble and she smells it coming our way. For all kinds of reasons that have to do with *other* people, I can't continue. I mean, Vogel is banging some married guy and the whole world knows about it, but you'd be robbing the cradle."

"Well, we'll just have to be good friends then. Love without sex. Let's see how we do," she said. We sat staring at the heater for a long, long time. We sat horny, silent, and sad.

I was angry as I left Gloria's apartment and drove home. I had let go of someone who loved me—someone who brought nothing but goodness into my life. We wouldn't finish what we had started. She left the following year for a teaching assignment in Michigan. For a short time we stayed in touch with letters and phone calls, but as time went by, our connection faded with distance and doubt and we moved on to new partners. I never found anyone like her. But then how could I? She was my other half.

As for Connie Vogel, she ended up marrying Paul Fulker after his wife died, and lived happily ever after.

20.

Mr. Spock

I WOULD turn nineteen in a few months and for the most part I had still not found life's silver lining. I began to cycle between disinterest, disenchantment, and anger. I wonder if this isn't the progression for all adolescent boys as they mature. As their eyes begin to open. First they are lost, then they become found, then they realize they were better off lost and get pissed off about it. I was beginning to receive too much information and it was guiding me to the conclusion that life was filled with double standards—good people die, lovers lose, and God most certainly did not answer prayers. This blur and my inability to sort through it made me feel as if an alien had slipped into my skin and was now inhabiting me.

I was easily hurt. I still worked hard at being the perfect student and son, while wanting to find my own unique freedom. I searched for a fortification against these numinous waves of emotion. Some bulletproof armor that would protect me from my father's anger, disapproval, and invisibility. My answer came one night watching *Star Trek*.

There he called to me, as he sat next to Commander James T. Kirk, the Vulcan called Spock. He didn't sweat the small stuff. He was a guy the unruly Klingons could ridicule and humiliate, but whose armor never got dented. He was one very cool, smooth alien dude and with him as my guide, I would train to withstand my father's bad manners and get a grip on myself.

In spring the aisles that ran through the mink sheds became muddy. The passage down the middle row was narrow, and navigating feeding carts or wheelbarrows was done carefully so as not to knock off or dent protruding aluminum water cups from the minks' cages.

A common springtime chore was to load a wheelbarrow with four hundred pounds of gravel, roll it down the aisles, flipping and tipping it into the spots that were soft and soggy. The flip and tip was done in one quick smooth motion while rolling forward at a steady pace.

Each would result in a small pile of gravel that would later be raked to fill in and groom the soggy spots.

I was one-hundred-seventy pounds of lean, solid muscle. I worked as hard as any man. One day, as I ran the wheelbarrow, dispensing gravel and grooming the center aisles, I fumbled my grip, dumping the wheelbarrow and ripping a number of cups off their cages. "Shit! What the hell is wrong with you! How many times have you done this! Look at the mess you've made!" my father shouted at me from the front of the misguided gravel pile.

I never yelled back, but this time I didn't turn and walk away. I had done my homework. I was prepared and stood my ground. I said nothing and stared. Spock had taught me that the key to this kind of warfare was not to blink. One had to have a clear placid mind. Like the Vulcans, I was now the master of my emotions. I stood there holding my feelings down. My chin did not tremble. I didn't turn or move. I burned a hole in him. After waiting a minute for my apology or my tears, my father sensed, but did not comprehend, that his son had been *Vulcanized*.

The Vulcan nation now stood behind their adopted son. As my power grew, I could feel my father's discomfort. But I was not about to let weeks of practice go to waste.

I stood and stared. At high noon, before three hundred blinking feline eyes, we stood face to face, repeating the age-old battle for male supremacy. We weren't beating our chests or butting our heads, but we were fighting it out. Like gunslingers we waited to see who'd blink first. Who'd back down? He finally moved and looked away, turning and telling me to "just clean this mess up." He walked away and did not look back. I didn't move until he was out of the shed and felt a piece of my budding personality lock firmly into place. I would never share myself with him again. That part of our life together was over.

. . .

I had completed a paper for my social studies class on the Geneva Accords. The hypothesis of my work was that the United States had broken international law by entering into a war with Vietnam. My usual instructor was sick on the day my paper was to be presented and our class was left in the hands of the assistant principal, a short, bald, and portly gentleman named Glen Yogadinski. We nicknamed him "The Tomato" because of his beet-red face, which boiled to a full glorious crimson when he lost his temper—something he did with great frequency for someone who should have been accustomed to the behavior of high school students. While my regular instructor liked my argumentative nature, The Tomato hated it.

"So in conclusion, the United States is engaged illegally in a war in Vietnam and in contradiction to the Geneva Accords. The U.S. government is killing innocent people; we are losing hundreds of American lives each day— young men are being drafted to fight in an illegal war. The United States must withdraw its forces from Vietnam now. Furthermore, it is my strong recommendation that every draft-age American male run to Canada or declare themselves objectors in conscience," I rambled on, making points on top of points. I had shot the U.S. government with one hundred bullets and wasn't done yet. In the back row of the classroom, I noticed a beacon of red crimson beginning to glow—The Tomato was rising. The warning light had been switched on. But I wasn't about to slow down and proceeded full speed ahead. Any tomato that got in my way was going to be pasta sauce.

"That will be just about enough out of you, Mr. Ries. You can sit down. I think you've made your point and said quite enough for one day. Frankly, you don't know what you're talking about. You're peddling a lot of rubbish. This is a great country and every student in this classroom knows it. Everyone, apparently, but you. We're not in Vietnam illegally and anyone who says we are has a few screws loose or is so far to the left, he should live in Russia. Are you a Russian, Mr. Ries, or an American?"

"Do you want me to read the accord to you right now, Mr. Yogadinski?" I had him on the ropes. It was a fair fight. The ignorant little prick was going down. "I have it right here. Let's see what my fellow students say about whether we're breaking international law," I said.

"I told you that would be enough out of you for today," he said, his head about ready to blow. My classmates and I could already see the walls awash in tomato sauce. He was down for the count. Still I couldn't let him up. If he was going to call me a lefty, then he'd better beat me with information. I knew my subject. I danced circles around him. I was about to fire my final shot when he said, "Get out of here. Get out now! We don't need your lies. Get out of here!" he shouted.

"Where do you want me to go—to the vegetable patch or the principal's office?" I replied in an untroubled tone.

"I don't care where you go. Just get the hell out of here," he roared.

I left the class halfway through the period and went

to the refuge of all nomadic intellectuals, lost prophets, and smart shits—the men's john. As I entered I was pleased to find Rick Beyer having a cigarette. "What are you doing here? Reading the graffiti?" I asked. Rick was tall, lean, and non-athletic. He was another member of the disenchanted elite who'd already received a full scholarship to a prominent eastern university and no longer thought high school was relevant.

"Crazy Connie asked for a paper comparing two great contemporary authors. So I took Henry Miller and compared him to Anaïs Nin. To make a point, I selected a few tasty pages from Henry Miller's *Tropic of Cancer*. You should have seen Vogel—I thought she was going to pass out from gasping. I don't think she's ever had sex in her life, which, as we both know, is entirely possible. You don't think she's really doing it with Fulker, do you? Pretty scary. Maybe I should have mooned the class for extra credit. Poor woman, her mind's been washed away by too many episodes of *The Flintstones* and *I Love Lucy*," he went on.

"Hey, you two give it up. This is high school. Stick with beer and sex," came a voice from a stall at the far end of the men's room. "Don't fight it; surrender. They're too many of them. They like things the way they are.

You'll feel better once you're drunk. I always do," the voice continued as a cloud of smoke billowed over the top of the closed door.

"So who's handing out free advice behind door number five?" Rick asked.

"None of your business. Just think of me as the smartest guy taking a crap you two will never meet," the voice answered.

"We've got to join forces. We're smarter than those sleep walkers," Rick said, trying to convince the voice to join our truth and liberation party.

"What are you going to do? This is *high* school. So get high, get laid, and stop the struggle. The best thing the counterculture ever did was give us drugs and free love," the voice said as the bell rang and we were released from temporary confinement.

"You got it all wrong," Rick said.

"Sure, whatever. Have it your way. Live the headache. Adios, pathetic earnest brothers-in-arms," the voice said as we walked out the door into a river of students passing through the halls between classes.

. . .

That spring I filed for my Conscientious Objector

status. I had to prove to my local draft board that I was morally opposed to the war. If granted Conscientious Objector status I would be placed in some hospital as a nurse's aid and fulfill my military obligation as a civilian. To make my case, I secured letters from my sister, Sue, Father Brager, my theater instructor, and, of course, Gloria. I included copies of the draft counseling columns I'd written for the school newspaper and any other evidence I could scrounge up that would prove I was a lover and not a fighter.

It was late July. I had graduated from East the month before and was working for my father over the summer before heading off to college. I had completed my chores and got to the dinner table late. My preferred plan was to eat dinner after my parents, so I wouldn't have to see them, but tonight they were both lingering over dessert and talking. When I walked in, my mother got up to make me a plate of food and began to clear the table. The late afternoon sun was streaming through the small window that was just above the sink. The back screen door was letting a warm breeze through the kitchen and the yard was alive with birds chirping as the day wound down.

"Mom, I need you to write a letter supporting my request to be a Conscientious Objector to the war," I said as I picked through my meal. I hated to ask my parents for help. The estrangement between us had grown. We'd run out of things we shared in common. Since graduation, I'd let my hair grow and assumed the uniform of a hippie in making. If we could survive until I went away to college in August, we'd all be better off.

My father never commented on the war or the draft. He read the paper, watched the news at night, and saw Jim and John avoid service through a series of student deferments. I had no idea where he stood on the matter. He wasn't in love with my long hair, tattered bellbottom jeans, or my political activism. They embarrassed him. Looking good mattered to my father. His children were an extension of him. I could be an ax murderer as long as my hair was short and I went to church on Sunday.

"Are you sure you want to do that? The war is winding down, you might never get drafted if you pull a good number," she replied.

"I don't want to take any chances. It would really help if I could get a letter from you."

"And say what?"

"Just say you know I'm a good kid and I'm opposed to the war. Tell them I've always been opposed to the war on moral principle."

"Maybe you could write a few paragraphs for me and…" my mother said, as my father interrupted.

"You're an American. You'll go to war if you're drafted."

I was silent. I didn't want a fight with him. "Dad, just support me in this. I'm not doing anything illegal. I can't fight in that war and you know it."

"You'll go if you're drafted. You'll serve your country."

"You don't have a clue what you're talking about. You didn't go to war—World War II, Korea, you never served. What do you know about any of this?" I shot back.

I wasn't sure why he was talking with me or why he was taking an interest in anything to do with me. Then I realized his concern wasn't about me—he didn't want to be embarrassed. He didn't want a story in the newspaper telling the world his son was a coward.

"Shove your war. I'm not going. If you want to fight, why don't you go? In fact, if you want to kill something, why don't you go out there and knock off of a few of your precious mink. Killing is killing, isn't it?" I pushed my chair back, stood up, and pointed to the mink yard that was framed by the large picture behind him. "You sit in that chair my entire life and never say a word and now you think you have a vote? You must think you have something to say about this? Well, the election's over and you lost. I'm not going to Vietnam. You can go to hell for all I care." My chin began to tremble and my throat tightened.

My words had landed dead center. He stood up and moved toward me.

"You're no son of mine. You're some kind of crazy kook! Look at you in that clown's outfit. You're an embarrassment!" he shouted.

As I took a step toward him, my chair clattering to the floor, my mother jumped in front of me. Her face was filled with hurt and fear. She never disagreed with my father. None of us did. She did everything to create peace and harmony. While she too had her doubts, she wouldn't desert me. I was her son.

"Stop this. What's the matter with you? Your father's worked hard his whole life for you. You just calm down," my mother said, pleading with me to not go any further with this discussion. "Go to your room. Quick. I'll write your letter. Now go." I stood a moment longer and glared at him over the top of my diminutive mother's head. I wanted to punch the dumb shit. *Why would he think me a coward and a clown? How could he want me to go to war?* I stared at him and begged him to step closer. I would push the dumb fucker through the picture window and pay him back for his years of indifference. He would learn that it was *he* who didn't matter.

I slammed the kitchen door behind me, ran to my truck, and drove around town for an hour, finally parking and sitting on the bluff overlooking North Beach. *What the hell do you want me to do? Who do you want me to be?* I asked, but the voices were quiet.

My father and I never talked about what happened that night. We unofficially agreed to tolerate each other. He was a man of principle, who tried hard to do the right thing, but he wasn't a fighter and neither was I.

21.

Night Crawlers

MY MOTHER was the very model of grace under fire. Women of less stature would have crumbled under the burden she carried—tending to seven children, working on the mink farm, participating in church work, and being married to a solid good-hearted guy who wasn't much fun. During the occasional moments of near meltdown, she would often say, "If it weren't for the church, you kids would be dead." We didn't quite understand what she meant by this, but were glad for whatever solace the good Mother Church brought into her life and prevented our untimely executions.

A month after our fight in the kitchen, my parents took their yearly summer road trip with Father Weller in his new set of wheels. Despite hating how I dressed, having serious doubts about my lifestyle and politics, my dad still trusted me with his mink. He didn't care that his son was a hippie; he still thought that I might have the knack and disposition to inherit his empire. I didn't have the heart to tell him he had staked his hope on the wrong son.

I took their departure as an opportunity to invite friends for a pre-college beer party. My plan was to have a few guys over, get drunk, and be done with it—nice and simple. My associates felt something grander was called for. They argued that I owed it to them for all the parties they'd hosted when their parents had left town. They assured me that everything would be fine and, after fifteen seconds of soul searching, I agreed.

I got a half-barrel of beer, put it in the outdoor feed cooler to chill, and waited for my ten buddies and a few girlfriends to join me. The first guests started to arrive just as I finished my chores at 5:00 p.m. and didn't stop arriving until well past 8:00 p.m. The word had gotten out. The hole in the party dam had gone from a trickle to a deluge. Ries wasn't having a party; he was having *the* party.

It didn't take long for our long gravel driveway to fill with cars, prompting late arrivals to park alongside the two-lane country trunk road that ran adjacent to our farm. The beer helped steady my growing anxiety and cloud my good judgment. Without it I might have thought, *this is becoming more than I bargained for.* The bedrooms were booked solid. Even my parent's bedroom was being used, "Guys, this is my *parents'* bedroom. Okay? I mean this is my parents' bedroom," I explained.

"It's a bed—a bed's a bed. What do you think God made beds for? Sleeping?" came the muffled, panting reply from two rolling mounds beneath the sheets, on the bed where I was conceived.

"There you are. What the hell you doing in here? Catching some live entertainment? Now you just get your drunken ass downstairs," a stumbling classmate said as he guided me back to the basement. The party continued to speed its way rapidly downhill until one of my guests called me from the kitchen, "Ries, there's some old fart here. He's looking for you."

"What'd you tell him?" I shouted back.

"I told him no Chucky Ducky Ries lives here."

"And then what did he say?"

"He said, he still wanted to see Chuck Ries. I guess the old geezer's deaf or something."

"What did he tell you his name was?"

"Ah, I think it's Uncle Pete, or maybe it was Fresh Meat," he laughed loudly. "At least I think that's what he said. Ya, that's what he said. He said, tell Chucky his Uncle Fresh Meat is here and Chucky Ducky better get his drunken butt outside on the double," he rambled on to the raucous laughter of the other drunks who were taking turns with me doing beer shots from the keg and passing joints around the holy circle.

In my joyful haze, I realized I had not considered the possibility of my Uncle Pete coming out and looking for night crawlers. Night crawlers are the big brothers of earthworms and a favorite fish bait of my uncle. As the name suggests, they came out at night and seemed to flourish under our mink pens, in particular, where the ground was always damp and the soil loose. One could walk with a flashlight down the aisles and pluck up enough to fill a good-sized coffee can. I ran upstairs to meet the *old fart* in the kitchen.

"Hey, Chucky, guess I picked good night to come looking for crawlers. I ought to get at least a can full," he said, as if he didn't notice the cloud of pot smoke, booming music, and the crowd of drunken revelers.

"Yes, well, sure, it does seem like a great night to get worms. Need any help?" I tried.

"Ries, just tell the old fart to get lost and get your ass back down here. It's your turn," a voice called from the basement.

"That's okay," my uncle replied. "I'm pretty sure I can handle this assignment on my own. Besides, your reflexes might be just a bit slow under the circumstances. I'll make a deal with you. You clear this place out by the time I get my worms and we'll have a talk. You got that?" he said, and went off into the night in search of worms.

"The party is over! My Uncle Pete's here," I shouted, and for good measure yelled, "he's called the cops." The word cops was like dropping a can of Raid in a cockroach hotel. The drunken bugs fled into the night and in ten minutes the house was cleared, quiet, and cluttered with beer cups, cigarette butts, and roaches. I stepped outside to the back porch, sat on the steps and waited for the return of my uncle.

Pete emerged out of the evening mists wearing his trademark Kingsbury Beer baseball cap and carrying a coffee can full of crawlers. As he sat down next to me he said, "Hey, Chucky, just look at this, I really landed some beauties. Those perch better watch out," he said, letting me look into the can as if it were filled with gold coins. "You know what these would cost me at the Ed's Bait

Shop? Four bucks. Do you have any idea how many fish I'll get with these? Ries Night Crawlers, the fisherman's friend. I don't know what it is about this place, but the ground under those pens is like a fertility clinic for worms. I never saw so many. Hell, I was grabbing four at a time."

"Not bad, Uncle Pete. Those worms didn't have a chance. I should've warned them you were coming, but you didn't call first," I mumbled, as I prepared for the punishment that was soon to befall me.

"Pretty quiet around here all of sudden," he said. "How're you doing? Your mom tells me you had a little brush up with your dad the other day?"

"Yup."

"She said she hopes you're doing okay and keeping out of trouble. She worries about you."

"I'm fine."

"I know that. Look, life is a kick in the shorts some days. But all in all it's pretty good. After what I went through in the War, I wouldn't want anyone to go fight unless they had to. Unless it was for a good cause. I'm not sure about this one, Chucky. But you're a good kid. You've always been a good kid. Nothing wrong with a little wild time. I had mine and you gotta have yours. But you gotta know your dad doesn't mean anything when he gets on you. He's not much fun, that's for sure, but he's a good man. He works hard and there's nothing wrong with that. Hey, some days you teenagers are a real pain in the butt, you know. As for me, I'd rather fish more and work less. But, hey, each to their own. Right?"

"I hate him."

"No, you don't. Not really. You're angry with him. But you don't hate him. Hating people just slows you down. Get angry and get over it. Got any free beer in there? I could sure use a tall one. And while you're in there, turn off the backyard lights. I want to show you something."

I brought two beers outside and sat next to him. Side by side, we drank in silence and, as our eyes adjusted to the darkness, we stared out over a lawn filled with so many fireflies it was as if we were adrift in a sea of stars. I'd thought about what he'd told me as we watched the fireworks twinkling around us. He leaned gently into my shoulder giving me support and, of course, having his free beer.

"One night in northern France, I was on guard duty with a guy in my platoon. It was a night a lot like this one. Warm, humid, quiet—the fireflies were all over the place. He was a big black guy from Mississippi. Nice guy—I think his name was Dwight Smith. A close friend of Dwight's was killed a few days earlier. The war was wearing him down. It was wearing us all down.

"'Peter, I think there's no God. No God would allow any of this to happen,' Dwight told me. 'I'm a good Baptist. Been good all my life. Praying hard, being as good a man as I know how to be. But damn this war has taken all the God and goodness out me,' and he began to weep and started to pray.

"Now, if you know any good Baptists, you know they can really pray," my uncle went on. "I tell you, Catholics could learn a thing or two about praying from the Baptists. Dwight gave it all he had.

"'Just let me know you're here, Lord. Just show me your love,' I heard him whisper.

"I let him be and didn't make anything of it. Well, after about five minutes, those damn fireflies started blinking in complete harmony. It was like God had given Dwight a light switch. For as far as we could see, those bugs were blinking on and then off, then on and then off. Dwight got the answer he was looking for."

"Cool story," I said.

"True story. You gotta have faith," Pete said. Faith that God's right there with you. Putting you right where you need to be. Giving you all you need. Some days are going to be tough, but other days you're going to see miracles. Signs that God is behind an invisible curtain that's hanging right here in front of us."

It had been quite a night.

"I'll make a deal with you. You never have another party like this and I won't tell your folks what happened tonight."

"Thanks. It was a dumb idea. It got out of hand. I didn't think it was going to get so big."

"Yup, you were dumb today. But you and your dad don't need another reason to get into each other's hair. So, no more parties. You got that?" he said.

"Got it."

"Good. You want to go fishing tomorrow? I'll come by about 4:00 a.m.? Have you back in time to start work at 7:00 a.m."

"You mind if I pass? I got some cleaning up to do."

"Well, maybe next week," he said, putting his arm around me. "You're a hell of a kid. You know your mom and I are close as can be. Best friends there ever were. She only has great kids. You know that, don't you?"

"I suppose. But some days I don't know shit."

"Well, that's not going to change. You just keep doing

what you feel is right," Pete said. "And speaking about doing the right thing, how about you getting your uncle a refill and he'll be on his way home."

I brought Pete another beer and a bonus bag of pretzels. He got up, walked to his car, and drove off into the night with his can of crawlers and our secrets.

22.

Black River

AS I ENTERED the third of a four-hour meditation, my legs began to cramp and my back ached. My mind continued to run in circles, but slowly it came to a standstill when for a long calm clear moment I saw him. I saw my father sitting next to me. He wasn't the father I'd known, but a Hindu monk. He was young, with a shaved head, but I distinctly knew it was my father and it dawned on me that prayer and service had not been enough to keep him in heaven. God had played a cruel trick on him when He made him return as a parent. What the monastery couldn't do, we his seven children, would. We'd grind his ego, temper, and impatience to powder and send him back to God without a blemish. In a flash the vision was gone. I'd seen him. I'd known my father before, as a monk. And when I found him again in this life, he was still a monk. *Perhaps parenting, not the priesthood is the path to God*, I thought.

So many stories. So many memories.

During the vigil prior to my father's burial, I walked up to his open coffin and slipped in an envelope filled with rose petals I'd been given years earlier after completing an advanced yoga training. I had left Catholicism long ago (if anyone ever truly leaves Catholicism) and was determined, through therapy and spirituality, to heal myself. I worked with a Jungian therapist to understand the meaning of my dreams. I studied Buddhism and Hinduism. I even traveled to North Africa to learn the mystical teachings of Islam. I left no rock unturned in my search for happiness. I discovered that when I calmed my mind, my thoughts became less self-critical. It wasn't perfect, but it was better.

That evening I drove out to where the mink farm had been. The sheds were now gone and the massive yard that housed our ten thousand animals had been replaced with a Super K-mart and a Piggly Wiggly. But the house my father and his brothers built sixty years before was still standing. My cousin Joan who, after a difficult divorce, needed a place to stay at a good price, was now renting it. My parents did what they'd always done and practically gave it to her. She was, after all, family.

As I glided to a stop on the gravel drive leading to my parents' home and climbed out of my car, Joan was already waiting for me on the back porch. "Hey, cousin, mind if I sit back here for awhile and think? I could always see further when I sat back here," I said as she reached out to give me a knowing embrace.

"Sure thing. You want a beer to keep you company?" she asked. "Hey, your dad was a good man. He just didn't have much to say. He came from a generation of silent men. Men who didn't burden others with their feelings. He showed his heart in other ways."

"Right. I know that."

Joan looked at me for a moment longer and then turned to go inside. When she returned she handed me a bottle of Kingsbury and gave me another long hug as I struggled to fight back a rising wedge of emotion.

My father was a hard guy to figure and, although I'd worked hard to forget him, he remained a primary suspect in the emotional arch of my life. I'd become a sweet, silent middle-aged man—successful, spiritual, and divorced twice with two teenage daughters. I'd worked hard to know about life, to understand how it worked, and yet I was still subject to sweeping self-doubt and sadness.

As I sat looking east from the back porch, I again tried to remember my life. I heard nothing but the crickets and the occasional car passing by. I thought about my father who'd be buried the next day and I longed for the kind of sustained joy that I'd read about in Buddhism or the here-today zest that I saw in my Uncle Pete and his children. But I realized I was not one who could sustain long joyous flights. I was a careful, thoughtful, plodder, just like my old man. I was a Ries.

And a final memory came to me.

It was the dead of winter. The temperatures were far below zero and a deep blanket of snow covered the ground. I had come home from college to help with pelting. My dad and I continued to bump heads and argued from time to time. But generally we maintained our truce. I was surprised when he invited me to go on a walk with him. It was the height of pelting season, and he wanted to go for a walk—with me—go figure. *Maybe the old man's going to give me some sage advice. Finally the pearls of wisdom he's been storing up will be shared with me,* I thought.

It was just before dusk as we drove the pick-up a

few miles south of Sheboygan and parked it alongside a county trunk road that crossed over the Black River. Wearing thick winter gloves, boots, jackets, and wool hats we got out and jumped down a slight embankment that led to the snow-covered surface of the river and began to walk side by side. First one hour going up the river and then an hour going down the river. The trees groaned as the wind gently moved them and our boots crunched the fresh dry snow. We walked through rolling hills, silent tree groves, and open fields. Beneath a slate gray sky, we saw no one, not a bird or an animal. We just walked; keeping our thoughts locked inside. When we arrived back at the truck we lifted our silence up into the cab and drove home. There would be no pearls of wisdom today.

"How was your walk?" My mother asked as we entered the back hall, stomping the snow off our boots and removing our coats.

"Well, it was fine. We had a good walk and nice talk, didn't we Chuck?" my father replied.

"Everything's cool, mom. Dad and I did some big time male bonding," I told her. She smiled with relief. She was pleased to know her husband had taken time to be with her son.

Our walk was one of his gifts to me. He'd reached deep within himself and told me he loved me. It was a grand gesture from a silent man, and it was good enough. There are the parents we are given, and the parents we find. We are shaped by all of them. After years of prayer, God had given me my miracle. A parade of angels disguised in baseball caps, floral skirts, and bib overalls had conspired to convince me that I was enough.

There are days I wish I could leave the small boy within me behind. To finally stop feeling the yearning and disquiet he felt. But none of us ever truly outgrow our childhood. We have the option to understand it and embrace it. We can learn to view this life as half-full and say, "God only gives us what we need, so bless what we've been given." But even with years of therapy, hours of meditation and the love of friends, we are, in the end, all a bit of that child who believed in angels, saw ghosts in the shadows, and worked just as hard as he could to find love.

END

A CITIZEN philosopher, Charles Ries was born in Sheboygan, Wisconsin. He lived in London and North Africa after college where he studied Sufism, the mystical teachings of Islam. In 1989 he worked with the Dalai Lama on a program that brought American religious and psychotherapists together for a weeklong dialogue, in Newport Beach, California. It was during this week that the Dalai Lama was awarded the Nobel Peace Prize.

Ries has done extensive work with men's groups and worked with a Jungian psychotherapist for over five years. During that time, he learned to find meaning in small things. He is also trained as a third degree Reiki healer.

Ries' narrative poems, short stories, interviews, and poetry reviews have appeared in over two hundred print and electronic publications. He is the author of seven books of poetry, including his latest publication, *Girl Friend & Other Mysteries of Love*. Ries has received five Pushcart Prize nominations for his writing, and was awarded the Wisconsin Regional Writers Association "Jade Ring" Award for humorous poetry. Ries is the former poetry editor for Word Riot, former member of the board at the Woodland Pattern Book Center, Co-Chairman of the Wisconsin Poet Laureate Commission...and founding member of Lake Shore Surf Club, the oldest fresh water surfing club on the Great Lakes. His work is archived in the Charles P. Ries Collection at Marquette University (*www.marquette. edu/library/archives/Mss/CPR/CPR-main.shtml*). You may write to him at: *charlesries@wi.rr.com*.

Praise For
The Fathers We Find

"Few authors capture the narrative voice with the perfect balance of self-deprecating humor and poignant insight that Charles Ries brings to *The Fathers We Find*. Ries' account of a small-town farm boy set against the backdrop of the Civil Rights Movement and the Vietnam War combines humor and heart to create a truly remarkable novel. The narrator stumbles his way to enlightenment with help from a series of delightful men on a journey that is hilarious and nostalgic."

–Camille N. Cline, Editor-in-Chief
The Literary Spa

. . .

"Charles Ries' story of his youth and family life is filled with colorful characters, evocative details, episodes both harrowing and humorous, and subtle wisdom. Every family –every life– should have a chronicler as honest, clear-eyed, and loving as Charles Ries."

–Larry Watson, Author *Montana 1948*

. . .

"Funny, fearless and fast. This spirited life-with-father reverie spins love, pain, and coming-of-age with skill and wit."

–Linda Aschbrenner, Editor *Verse* Poetry Magazine

. . .

"Ries gives us wonderful insight into small-town American life…and a beautiful understanding of why we are who we are."

–Patty Johnson

. . .

"The father-son relationship can be very difficult. It has changed through the years but in 'our era' it was often painful. I have four brothers. I will have them read this book…"

–Mary Evans

. . .

THE FATHERS WE FIND

"*The Fathers We Find* exposes you to worlds you haven't experienced and makes you aware you are not alone in this journey."

–Mary Kay Ring

. . .

"Charles Ries' novel reminds me of Frank McCourt's *Angela's Ashes* and *'Tis Teacher Man* memoirs with their keen attention to character and strong voice. Ries' characters' voices ring loud and clear, I can hear them calling, long after putting the book down. When characters follow me for days after reading, when I'm sad to see the story end, I know this is true."

–Karla Huston, Author *Inventory of Lost Things*
Winner of *Main Street Rag* Poetry Book Competition

. . .

"You have me filled with the thoughts of those lessons that we all learn when we don't really know we're learning them. I did not know I was reading a great book until I was silently yanked in by the characters—and then I looked back and wondered how I got there."

–Tracy Weyers

. . .

"I can't remember the last time I laughed or giggled while reading. I was laughing near tears with this novel. Seeing the world through Chuck's naive but watchful eye was just wonderful."

–Michelle M. Bria, CEO Journey House

.   .   .

"Wow! I have read many thousands of novels, for years and years that's all I did, and I have to say, Charles' story ranks up there with any book I've ever read. It's so honest and beautiful and poignant."

–Peter Schwartz, Author
My Novena and *The Nowhere Glow*
Associate Art Editor for *Mad Hatters' Review*

.   .   .

CPSIA information can be obtained at www.ICGtesting.com
Printed in the USA
LVOW06s0623151015

458342LV00002B/2/P